CW01046471

Brannie Jackson's love of life, thirst for knowledge and a consuming desire to leave behind a previously miserable and limiting life existence, in search of the completely happy and purposeful life she believed was possible, led to her reading psychology, science and spiritual books in preference to fiction from a young age. Later on, she trained as a counsellor, reiki master, meditation teacher and TEFL teacher, and has dedicated her life to the pursuit of understanding the potential of the unique space we humans occupy in this marvellous universe of ours. Her greatest wish and desire is to share her amazing and enlightening experiences and stories with the rest of the world in the hope that these may serve to inspire and assist others on their own unique and personal journeys of discovery, as they too search for the happiness and life they personally desire. *Chasing Happy* is written from a place of true care, love and light, that will hopefully touch the hearts and minds of its precious readers.

For my beautiful, brilliant and amazing daughter Melanie, who kick-started my search to be a better person. Love you to the moon and back always.

For GB, you live in my heart, thank you.

For Izzy, Ruth, Manuel, Andrea, Julia, Lucia, Sharon Seider, Laurie Allard, Lourdes Gassin with love and friendship.

For Lesley Anne, we are all each other's teachers, and thank you.

For Frank, Morag, and all of the special and beautiful members of my Silver Coast meditation group, as well as all of my other lovely friends and family, and especially my wonderful, loving and supportive husband Paul! Thank you. I love you all.

Brannie Jackson

CHASING HAPPY

AUSTIN MACAULEY PUBLISHERS™

LONDON • CAMBRIDGE • NEW YORK • SHARJAH

Copyright © Brannie Jackson 2022

The right of Brannie Jackson to be identified as author of this work has been asserted by the author in accordance with sections 77 and 78 of the Copyright, Designs and Patents Act 1988.

All rights reserved. No part of this publication may be reproduced, stored in a retrieval system, or transmitted in any form or by any means, electronic, mechanical, photocopying, recording, or otherwise, without the prior permission of the publishers.

Any person who commits any unauthorised act in relation to this publication may be liable to criminal prosecution and civil claims for damages.

The story, experiences, and words are the author's alone.

A CIP catalogue record for this title is available from the British Library.

ISBN 9781398434714 (Paperback)
ISBN 9781398434721 (ePub e-book)

www.austinmacauley.com

First Published 2022
Austin Macauley Publishers Ltd®
1 Canada Square
Canary Wharf
London
E14 5AA

My undying thanks to Austin Macauley Publishers for daring to demonstrate faith and support of a new writer's first book, especially when it is outside of mainstream fiction! And, for granting my dearest wish in sharing *Chasing Happy* with the world!

Friends, Izzy and Brannie, chatting together as friends do and debating life.

"So who am I?" asks Brannie. "I know my name and I know my roles in life; I'm a mum, a daughter, a sister, and a friend, and I know what I *do* every day. But that's not actually *ME,* is it? Who and where am *I*? (Patting her body) I mean, If someone opened my body up, they wouldn't actually be able to find *me* in here anywhere would they, and I know I'm not out there, outside of my body either. So then, where am I, where do I exist, and how do I go about finding me?"

"Mmm weird, huh. I've often wondered the same thing about myself," replied Izzy nodding seriously. "Scary thing is though, what if you don't like you when you find you!!! Perhaps you'd better not look!"

Table of Contents

Part 1
Looks At Life As We Know It

Preface
From Me to You

"Wherever you go, you take yourself with you.
So, find your happy space and live from there."
—Brannie Jackson

Dear Friends,

I write to you now from the deepest, most joyous well of happiness, hoping that it touches you in some way, and so helps you in finding it for yourself too. I am speaking of the kind and level of happiness that we all want to find and hope really exists out there somewhere, and I am here to tell you that it does. You are much closer to it than you think, and once you align with it, it will affect every area of your life in the most positive and amazing ways. It is with you right now just as it has always been, and simply needs to be revealed by you. It is yours alone and it really is all about you.

I sincerely hope and intend that *Chasing Happy* is a useful and helpful tool for you as you continue on your life journey's path and search for the happy life you desire and deserve.

Within the chapters and pages that follow you will also find three short 'stories' that are based upon and depict some of my most profound real-life experiences. I hope that they may serve to entertain, enlighten and inspire you to make the effort to align with who you really and naturally are. I know you will be so glad that you did. May you find the happy place that is your natural home and live the rest of your days from there.

It has been my absolute joy and privilege to teach and assist other searchers in growing and connecting with themselves to achieve the happiness in this life they seek. And I feel both blessed and humbled to be able to accompany you too, on your amazing journey of discovery as you learn how to live the life you dream of and desire!

I wish you love, light and much, much happiness!

Happy is so much closer than you think!

Brannie xx

Chapter 1
And so, It Began

Have you ever looked around yourself and thought that there's just got to be more to life than this? I did. Have you ever wondered why, despite you giving your best efforts at life in all its departments, it still always feels like there's something missing? I did, as did most of the other people I knew. Ever thought that 'completely happy' is really an illusory state of being that only exists and belongs in fairy tales? I did, and so did most of those other people. Well, I'm here to tell you now, that if that's true, you can call me Cinderella!

The saying goes that 'the darkest hour is just before the dawn', and my darkest hour was when I finally decided that I had just about had enough of constantly striving and giving my all, and still only managing to just about eke out a lack-lustre and stress filled living. I decided that 'there was a storm brewing with the winds of change'. I was taking no prisoners, and no-matter what my situation or life circumstances were, change was about to occur, and it was starting right here, right now. Other people could accept 'OK' as a fair description of the weather and the quality of their lives if they wanted to. I wanted more. I wanted happy. Not happy-ish. Not 'OK' kind of happy, but properly lush, all-consuming, sustaining and blissfully, completely happy. I believed it was out there and within my reach if I could just find it, and I intended to do just that. My search had begun!

I chose to ignore the derisive advice from my nearest and dearest to "stop chasing rainbows and looking for miracles". I didn't listen when they told me that I had delusions of grandeur because, "this is just how life is for everyone, it's normal, accept it. What's so special about you?". And, I refused to accept that the quality of my life was as good as it was ever going to be. I had listened to everyone else all my life and it had landed me right where I was here and now, which was precisely what I was going to change.

Crazy? My mother said so. But, I just knew that the kind of happiness and quality of life I was looking for was possible. I knew it was out there somewhere, and I knew that it wasn't about other people, or material 'stuff' and 'things.' It was all about me. I could feel it. I just needed to know how and where to find it.

You already know the ending to the aged-old fairy-tale. Cinderella got to live happily ever after. And, I did what I set out to do. It took me some time and a lot of searching, but I found Happy, that bright, shiny place that's always on our horizon, not too far away, but usually just out of reach for today.

I want to share my experiences and journey with you now, so that you too can find your Happy.

Happy hunting my friends!

Chapter 2
My Beliefs and What I Know

Having read chapter 1, you will have begun to realise by now that I don't generally take 'no' for an answer, or give-up very easily on anything! It's who I am. And, I'm here now to say that in complete opposition of how my mother felt about things or generally saw life and believed it to be, I remain very glad of my stubborn refusal to accept that my predictable future would play-out and reflect the hard, limited and uninspiring lives of the people in the world I then knew.

My unwavering belief in, and search for, the possibility of a completely fulfilling, purposeful and happy life here on planet earth, and the eventual amazing and gratifying realisation of it, is what brings me now, in the form of this book to you.

There's a saying that goes 'when the student is ready the teacher appears,' and I believe that we are all each other's teachers, in every moment of every day, and that our lives continue to unfold perfectly to meet our needs and requirements, except most of us aren't open to, and therefore sadly miss the messages and opportunities we might otherwise benefit from.

Science tells us that in our vibrational energy world there are natural laws, which everything in the universe accords and complies with as a matter of course, one of which is 'like unto itself is drawn,' popularly referred to these days as the Law of Attraction. Which latter means basically that what you give out, you get back, not as a reward, or as a punishment, but simply in accordance with the flow of the natural laws, which tell us that nothing ever happens co-incidentally or by chance, and that we are all co-operative components in every given situation. Therefore, if you're reading this book, it's because it has a message just for you, and it also means that you are ready to receive it.

The way I see it, I am not here to argue for my point of view. I don't need to. I know my own power and truth. It's for you alone to know yours. Neither am I here to tell you what to do, or to guide your life experience so that it is directly in line with my own, in the belief that I have all the answers to all the questions. That I am the only one who knows what's right, and that everyone else should try and copy my life experience and believe exactly as I do. Far from it. I just want to help you understand, believe and come to know that you are the Creator of your own experience, as I am the Creator of mine. I just want, through the clarity of my own example, to facilitate your awakening and recognition of the powerful and beautiful being that you really and truly are, and to guide you to find your own happy and amazing life of well-being that truly exists when you align with who you genuinely and naturally are.

And, for those doubters along the way, who might suggest that I am just a dreamer and don't want to face reality as it really is. My answer to that is 'I don't *face* reality at all, not any more. I *create* reality, and I love enjoying living the super-happy life I have created for myself. I love my life! I love myself! I am having the best time I've ever had and living the life I always dreamed of living! And, I'm really pumped and very excited about the future life that I am currently in the throes of planning and creating for myself too. How about you?'

The very fact that we are all of the same energy logically suggests that we are all equal. We are all as special, deserving, and worthy as each other. No-one is better, or of more value than another, no matter how much money, how many possessions or how much power they may appear to have to our materially minded society, where we've learned to mistakenly equate worth and value with money and position. We all have access to exactly the same limitless power and potential, and this becomes clearly demonstrated for us, once we understand who we really are, and break down the programmed barriers that have been constructed around us along the way and that do such a good job of holding us back.

Most of us know or feel that we have stores of untapped power, creativity and potential within us, but we have absolutely no idea of how to go about finding them. Happily for you my Friends, I have spent a lifetime looking for them so that you will not have to! I'm here to help guide you. Read on!

I believe that everything we see around us is a reflection of who we are, and that everyone of us has the ability to completely transform our lives if we just want to enough, and are willing to put the work in to achieve it. In fact, I don't just believe this. I know it for a fact, because I have done so personally and I've witnessed others do the same. So, if you're up-for-it let's take a trip to Happy and see how much better life can be!

Chapter 3
So, Who on Earth Are You?

Do you know who you are? I mean really, really, really know who you are? Well I'm going to hazard a guess that, like most of the human population, you don't actually have the answer to that one!

Sure, you know what you do, what your roles in life are, eg., mother, father, friend, lover, office worker, doctor, and on and on.

If you're someone that's done a lot of deep-thinking and work on themselves you might be more aware than most of your beliefs, values and personal characteristics, but they're not *you* are they? They're about what you think and what you feel.

If you opened your body up would you find *you*? No, you wouldn't, although you know you're in there somewhere. What you would find is lots of blood, along with your vital organs, muscles, tissues etc, and they're not you either. They're all part and parcel of your physical body, but they're not *you.*

So then, where are you, and, if you're inhabiting your physical body, how is it that you can't be found anywhere in it? For instance, a doctor could operate on your body-parts if necessary, but the same doctor wouldn't be able to operate on *you*, because, of course, they would have to locate you first in order to do so.

You may answer then that you can't be found in your body because you exist in your mind. Aaah, OK, so that's where you are then. That's where you can be found, right? No. Can't find you there either. Mind is energy and it generates energy. It uses the brain and the brain responds to the mind. Modern science simply lacks the tools to show the intangible essence that makes us human, and that is the entity that we call conscious self.

Ok, so you know that you exist. You experience the world around you subjectively through your thoughts, feelings, emotions and instincts and objectively through your physical body. How is it then that you cannot be found in a pretty little parcel existing somewhere within the confines of your physical body, in a pocket labelled as 'Me?' And the answer to that is; because you are a vibrational being! You are a vibrational energy being in a vibrational energy world and inhabiting what appears as a 'physical body.'

Not such a shock or so different from what we already accept and believe really, when you think about it, is it? When our loved ones pass from life in this 'physical' worldly realm, we believe and accept that they're no longer inhabiting what was their former body. Otherwise, we surely wouldn't agree to their being buried or cremated would we? No, of course not. We accept that the *person* we knew has gone. They've moved on and left their physical body behind. We have accepted that this is the case for aeons. We accept completely that the being we previously knew when they were 'alive,' inhabiting their body and moving around in it, was not actually a physical being after all and that they've moved on somewhere else. So logically, it can't really come as a total shock to us when science is in complete accord with this, and agrees that we are, indeed, vibrational energy beings can it? No, not at all. It's logical and it makes sense.

Science has proven and tells us that this world and everything in it is intelligent vibrational energy. Me, you, trees, mountains, fish, stones and even down to nanobes, the smallest known organisms. Everything!

Funnily enough, the scientific evidence and proof of our vibrational energy world apparently came off the back of scientists searching to prove exactly the opposite in the early 20th century by looking for the elementary 'point particle' upon which all life is built, and which would finally prove that 'reality' was not an illusion, and that the physical universe is, after all, actually physical.

What the scientists ended up proving instead, is that everything *is* energy at the most fundamental levels. And, when you think about it, and quite amazingly dear Friends, if everybody in the world understood and could get their heads around what science has proven about the energetic nature of reality, our planet would change overnight! Really!

So then, I hear you ask, 'what does this vibrational energy thing mean to each and every one of us? It's just science, why would we care?' Glad you asked. It means that we are here to create and mould energy into the lives we desire and want to live. It means that, in ignoring our true vibrational energy nature, we are currently only ever achieving a very tiny proportion of our enormous potential in life. It means that there is a very important part of 'us' and of our natural selves that's being laid-waste and unused and is missing from our daily lives. And it means that we really do have the potential to be so much more than we are right now! Amazing? Yes it is! This is exciting stuff and it's totally real! So start now on your search to find you! Time is a-wasting!

All you have to do on your incredible journey of discovery and in order to find out how beautiful, powerful and special you are, is to align with your true nature and natural self, which is with you now, just as it always has been. It's in the background lying quietly, patiently dormant, and just waiting to be revealed by you!

Wonderful isn't it, to know that this is all about you? You don't have to go anywhere, or do anything with, or according to, anyone else's ideas of who you are or what you should do. You can't fail, or get this wrong. You just have to want to make the effort to look for and reveal the spectacular being that you really are, and I know that you'll be so glad you did.

Your life is all about you! It's meant to be all about you. We are each individual and unique on purpose, and for good reason. Each of us has unlimited potential. Excited? You should be!

Are you ready to start your search?! Read on. I'll be right beside you.

ENERGY EXERCISE

Just by way of an energy demonstration, let's do a simple little exercise.

First, think of a scenario or something *unreal* that is sad. Take the time to picture it, think about it and feel it. You're likely to become aware that your shoulders and posture generally droop in response to your sad and negative thoughts and feelings. Your body will possibly feel heavier and you may be surprised at how quickly and easily your mood changes as you become more negative, unhappy and sad.

Next

Now, smile. Smile, as big as you can, even if you don't feel like smiling, and even if you feel silly doing so. Just do it anyway. You can smile at yourself in a mirror too, if you want to, mirror work can be very powerful. Feel how your mood is lifting. Feel how your body energy reflects your smiling and is almost instantly better, lighter and happier.

Remember that you're a vibrational energy being living in a vibrational energy world. As is everything, your thoughts are energy too, and you've just proven to yourself that they don't even have to be about anything apparently 'real' or already experienced by you, in order to affect you and effect change in your life. This is an example of how you're flowing both positive and negative energies throughout your day, without even being generally aware of doing so, and, of how powerful these energies are.

You've got far more input and control over your life than you currently realise or know. It's just up until now you've sort of lurched and almost stumbled into your life situations, mostly believing that life is out of your control and has happened to you, rather than because of you. Time to take back control and start living the life you want to live. Time to be your total Self and see just what you can accomplish when you are. Exciting!

Chapter 4
Chasing Happy

"If you want to realise your full potential
If you want to be blissfully joyously happy
If you want to manifest your dream life
If you want to be able to handle life's problems with ease
You first have to connect with who you really are!
Then, and only then, will you have everything you need to
create the life you want to live."
—Brannie Jackson

So what is happy? Well the dictionary definition of the word says it's feeling or showing contentment or pleasure. Just reflect for a moment and ask yourself how often you do either of these. How often have you felt contentment and pleasure today, or yesterday, or the day before? Most people I asked said that neither of the aforementioned are something they generally get the time to even think about, as they're too busy getting on with the stressful minutiae of everyday life!

We understand of course that happiness takes a variety of forms and means different things to different people. Most of us have an idea of, or can picture in our mind's eye what happy means to us personally. However, it's true to say isn't it, that for most of us, and most of the time, Happy is usually to be found 'hanging out' just over there on the horizon. It's that bright, shiny place we're consistently searching and heading for, that's often almost within our grasp and not too far away, but somehow always just out of reach for today. Never mind though. We console ourselves by thinking of the next holiday we're planning or the next time we're going to be doing something we like, and that'll make us happy, won't it? We all spend our lives looking to find and secure happiness and in the avoidance of pain. So then, why do we seem to be forever, consistently and persistently 'chasing after Happy'? What void are we trying to fill? What is it that's missing from our lives so that we have to continually forward plan to be happy?

Do you know of anyone who wants to be unhappy? No, of course you don't. Everything we do in life is geared towards making us happy in some way, i.e., going to good restaurants and eating food we enjoy. Buying clothes we love that make us feel good about ourselves. Getting a fab new hairstyle that makes us feel trendy and 'current.' Listening to our favourite music because it lifts our mood. Choosing people we like and have something in common with as friends. Getting a new job because it pays more and will enable us to have more of the things we like, etc, etc.

We know that happiness can take a number of different forms. For instance, who doesn't enjoy receiving lovely gifts? Personally, I can think of a long list of things that I would totally enjoy being given as a present, and as some of them filter across the cinema screen of my mind I find myself wondering whether it might not behove me to elaborate somewhat on said list. Just in case someone I know is reading this! Although, many of my dear friends are already aware and can attest to the fact that I do have a real 'thing' for properly lush and pillowy soft marshmallows! Which factor may well seem to be of little general significance or regard; however, for one who enjoys them immensely but resides in a place where it's impossible to purchase them, I must heartily disagree! As must I also sincerely thank my aforementioned friends for remembering, and also caring enough to renew my supplies often! You know who you are! I love you! Much appreciated. Anyway, I digress! We completely accept that the kind of happiness gifts bring is fleeting and ephemeral and most likely will unfortunately have dissipated before the gift gets old, (unless you've eaten it). This type of happiness is just about 'stuff'. It's sunshine through the clouds on a rainy day, in that it's lovely and thoroughly enjoyable but lasts just for a short period of time. It's not the lasting, deeply fulfilling and sustaining type of happiness that we privately long for and would love to have in our lives, but struggle in believing is an actual real possibility outside of movies or books.

We all want our lives to be better, but the problem is, we don't really believe they can be. Most of us simply accept the stressful and battering emotional roller-coaster of our lives because that's just how it always has been for us and for everyone else we know. It was that way for our parents, their parents and their parents before them; for our family, friends and work colleagues. Why should we be any different, after all what's so special about us? This is normal. It's how life is! Life's hard! Sure, happy happens sometimes, but usually by chance, by coincidence, by the law of averages, or, if you're just plain lucky and having a particularly good day. We all know that completely and blissfully happy only exists in stories and fairytales, don't we? Otherwise, wouldn't we already have experienced it for ourselves?

Generally, we look to the material world about us to provide our happiness. "We'll get to Happy when we get the perfect new job, buy the perfect new car or find our perfect new life partner or when…" Then the new job, the car and the life-partner turn out to be not so perfect, and the initial happy feelings fade, leaving us discontent and back 'on the road' and looking for Happy again. We're optimists though and can still see it on the horizon, "We'll get there if we keep trying. Happy's not too far away. We got it wrong last time, and the time before, and the time before that, but we'll do better next time, then we'll be happy."

Many people spend their entire lives searching for 'security' in some form or another, in the mistaken belief that they can find happiness through its attainment. Usually failing to realise their goal because there just never comes the time when they actually feel really secure or consider that they have enough of whatever it is they are seeking. And, even if they do, the dichotomy being that the future by its very nature, must always remain unknown and unrealised, and therefore insecure. Once again sending the seeker back 'on the road,' and searching for Happy.

We spend most of our lives chasing after happiness and more often than not, we are left wondering whether this elusive thing called 'happy' even really exists. For much or at least some of the time we are happy but not completely happy, satisfied but not completely satisfied, comfortable but not completely comfortable etc. There's always that niggling feeling and belief that there has to be something more. It's common for many of us to acknowledge experiencing feeling lost in an emotional wasteland of a real sense of lack, and as though something important is missing in our lives. This occurs even if and when, to an outsider's eye, we're apparently doing well and are seemingly happy, affluent and prosperous. That feeling that there's something missing and that we could have and be achieving more still remains.

So, with no inkling or understanding of exactly what the elusive missing piece in the puzzle is, we settle for continuing to do things the way we've always done them and paper over the cracks by buying some nice new things that make us feel happy for a little while, until we're bored with them when we'll repeat the process and replace them with other new things that might make us feel happy for a little while more.

We go through our days feeling positive and upbeat when we experience things we like, or negative and downbeat when we encounter things we don't. Our emotions are constantly up and down, and although this is stressful and it wears us out, we accept that this is just how things are because it happens to just about everyone we know. It's normal. This is life and it's as good as it gets. But is it? It doesn't have to be. It's not how it's meant to be. It's meant to be so much more.

The reason we so often feel like there's something missing; is because there really is! But, worry not. The good thing here is that it's not too far away. Everything you need to live the completely content and happy life you've always dreamed of is with you right now, you just need to look in the right place.

We are all amazing beings who deserve to be happy! We are meant to be happy! Our natural state of being IS happy! You just don't know it yet because you haven't looked in the right place for it. If you want to buy chicken and fresh vegetables for dinner tonight you wouldn't go to the nearest dress shop to buy them would you? No, of course not. That doesn't make sense, as the dress shop doesn't sell them and you won't find them there. Chicken and vegetables do exist; just somewhere else. You have to look in the right place!

HAPPY EXERCISE

Take a few minutes now, to think of something/someone or somewhere that makes you feel really, really happy and just bask in those enjoyable feelings for a while. Notice how your body responds to the happy sensations, and how much brighter, lighter and better your mood is when you stop.

Wouldn't you like to feel this way more often? Wouldn't you love to feel this way every day? Happy is your natural state of being, and once you align with who you really are, you can. Why spend another precious moment of your life ignoring your potential to be really and truly happy?

Life can be a wonderfully happy and fulfilling journey of continuous personal growth, creativity and achievement. It can be everything we want and all that we desire if we simply align with our innate beautiful self, instead of looking to all the wrong things and in all the wrong places for our happiness and contentment. Happy is 'hanging out' right where you are, right now. You just need to knock on the door, and *Chasing Happy* is going to show you how. Happy homecoming!

Chapter 5
Who Have You Learned to Be?

We have *learned* to become who we are, or more correctly, who we *think* we are, based on both our personal and cultural conditioning. We have formed a mental image of who we *think* we are and often we feel uncomfortable with this learned image and find it difficult to like, approve of and love ourselves. That's because we are trying to like, love and approve of a largely false, acquired version of who we really and truly are. Simple really.

At the beginning of your life journey, you existed happily at the very centre of your universe. You loved and liked you. You appreciated you. You were contented and full of love. You saw no frailties, weakness or dysfunction. You were at ease and totally comfortable with who you were then, and you were guided intuitively and always by your feelings. If you were comfortable and happy, you smiled and laughed, and if you were uncomfortable or unhappy, you cried, or shouted and drew attention to it, until the discord was resolved and perfect homeostasis was restored. You wanted, and expected to feel good. It was your right. It was how it was naturally meant to be. It is how it is still meant to be.

How about now? How much do you like or approve of yourself now? Can you honestly say that you love yourself? Are you the centre of your universe still, or are you flailing around with no real direction and lost apologetically in the background somewhere? How often do you find yourself feeling joyful? When was the last time you contentedly reflected upon how good your life is and how happy you are? If you're reading this book I'm guessing that it's not very often, or certainly not anywhere near as often as you would like. So what happened? How did you lose sight of happy? How did you lose sight of you?

From the beginning of our lives society gives us our 'idea' of who we actually are. We are told our name, where we live, where we belong on the social scale and what we are expected to achieve in the future. As children we are shown by example how to behave in order to fit into our familial and social environment and we learn very quickly that to step outside of these allotted parameters unleashes a backlash of displeasure and discomfort in a variety of ways that we don't, or won't enjoy.

So, like the good children we are, and even later on, as adults, we become adept at 'fitting in,' sometimes at great cost to ourselves and even when it feels unnatural and uncomfortable to us. We do it anyway. Much easier to simply do as we're expected to, and avoid dealing with the potential difficulties we might otherwise have to face. We become adept at 'putting on a brave face' to please those around us, so often and so much so, that it eventually simply appears as normal behaviour to us, and in time, we too begin to believe that this is really who we are. We learn to pretend, and then forget that we're pretending!

Silently, somewhat wistfully and privately we acknowledge to ourselves that no-one else truly knows who we are, or what we're all about. Everyone we know seems to have an idea of who they think we are though, and we go along with that, adapting our personal behaviour and even mannerisms, trying our hardest to 'fit in,' and to meet others expectations, so as to gain favour and be accepted, to feel validated, and to continue to belong. Human beings are pack animals and want to belong to their herd.

We wear ourselves out keeping everyone else happy as we ride our own personal emotional rollercoaster, continually behaving as we believe we are expected to, and giving our own power away to others in the mistaken belief that it will bring us happiness and security. So, when you think about it, it really is hardly surprising that we feel and eventually come to believe that we are powerless in our own lives, isn't it?

We're taught our parents opinions and world views that have been passed down from generation to generation. Many of the beliefs are outdated, heralding back from who knows where or when, and have deep-seated negative concepts about life and lack in general, that may have been appropriate at the time of their conception but often bear no real resemblance to our own lives today. Nevertheless we unconsciously and unquestioningly live by them, and we lose sight of our dreams as we mature and behave as we are expected to do.

We naturally emulate the people we grow up around, unquestioningly accepting their behaviour as 'normal' because that's all we know and have experienced. A quiet, well-mannered and soft spoken family are likely to produce quiet, soft-spoken and well-mannered children. Whereas a loud, aggressive family are more likely to produce loud and aggressive children. If you take a moment to think about your own family and friends you'll probably be able to identify a number of them who echo their parent's behaviour, mannerisms and life-styles.

It is common to find that a child from a brutal, bullying background will go on in later life to become a bully themselves. Or, a child from a background of alcohol abuse will also grow-up with alcohol related problems. Without even being aware of, or trying to, we learn to echo and 'fit-into' our environment, whether it serves our best interest well or not. Otherwise known as conditioning.

So often, those that we would suppose and expect to be the ones to know us best, appear to really know us the least. Those who have known us over a period of many years would have formed initial impressions of and about us, and those early implanted impressions often remain resolute, despite the fact that we may have made significant personal changes as we matured and experienced what life had to offer us.

Our familial and social environments envelop, instil and similarly colour the beliefs and values of all those who reside within their circles, whether or not these values serve a useful purpose or are even appropriate for the lives they affect. Sadly, thereby effectively blocking each individual's chances of future happiness and success.

Of course, our conditioning does not just emanate from what we hear and are told about ourselves, it develops through our direct experiences too. Our immediate environment is also partially instrumental in determining our own expectations of ourselves, our place on the social ladder of life and our potential possible futures as we observe the people and situations about us in our own particular corner of the world.

In our household it was expected that I would work in a shop, hairdressers or office for a couple of years, and then get married at a young age and have children. I didn't seem to figure much personally speaking in the equation and conclusions reached by my mother. There were no expectations of my studying further or having any sort of career. This was widely accepted as the general rule of thumb for girls around my age and from my type of working class background. My own friends all excitedly discussed with great enthusiasm which shops they wanted to work in. Fashion and hairdressers won by a country mile.

However, it was a completely different scenario for one of my school friends who lived close-by with her wealthy family (comparatively speaking, as ours was not a wealthy area). Right from babyhood, her family had determined that she would study hard, attend university and carve out a career for herself in music, emulating her own mother's achievements and in similar accord with the other members of that particularly musical family. I recall being invited to the girl's house to hear her play her flute and violin, so she was right on track to meet with family expectations, and indeed, she did go on to play with an orchestra. As you believe, so it is.

The early lessons we learn in life remain embedded in our psyche to rise up again and again in our future to inform and determine the person we currently believe ourselves to be, whether these values and beliefs be positive or negative and whether we like it or not. We become conditioned. For instance, someone who is often told when young that they are stupid, will eventually come to believe it to be true, and is very likely to have low self-esteem and limiting expectations of themselves that serve to block and hinder their successes in many areas of their future life.

As a teenager I had two girlfriends who were the exact opposites of each other. One, let's call her 'A,' was quite literally the prettiest girl I had ever seen. She was intelligent and personable, if a little reserved and closed-off emotionally. I admiringly thought that she was wonderful and had it all. However, her home life had been a difficult one, in that no-one had any time for her and so she had not learned to place any value or positive attributes to herself. In spite of her being really intelligent and absolutely gorgeous, she felt largely invisible and generally worthless. At school, due to her acting skills and partially down to her exceptional good looks 'A' was chosen from a vast number of other applicants to play the lead in our version of Romeo and Juliet, which for most people would have been a real confidence boost in itself, never mind the fact that she was playing opposite the school 'hunk' lucky girl! Not for her though. She couldn't see the accolade, and found a variety of reasons why she had probably landed the role by default. In the end, she delivered an outstanding performance, but sadly remained entirely deaf to the many resulting compliments showered upon her, appearing embarrassed by them and simply disbelieving, or just not hearing them. And more sadly than that, she even believed it possible that people were laughing at her instead! 'A' interpreted everything according to her learned negative beliefs about herself, thereby reducing even her demonstrated, actual positive outcomes and achievements to non-existent and negative. It grieves me to tell you that she continued on in this way for much of her adult life, and finally settled down with a man who also failed to see her magnificence and continued to treat her in the negative ways she had always known, accepted and come to expect. A naturally bright and shining star that never learned to sparkle!

The other girlfriend, 'B,' was short, chubby and quite plain featured and usually to be found with a huge grin on her face. She good-naturedly muddled her way through school, career and thereafter in many different life situations, always expecting everything to work out for her, as it usually did. 'B' heralded from a warm, happy and loving home, where she was constantly reminded of how valued and special she was. I can clearly recall her words when chatting with me one day about our friend 'A.' She said 'I know I'm not beautiful and clever like 'A' but, at least I'll always know that other people really want me for me.' How secure in herself and wise was she! I am happy to be able to tell you that she went on to be constantly promoted in her career and became very successful, probably more down to her easy-going and likeable character than proclivity to academia and business sense. And, she also bagged herself a wonderful man who loved, appreciated and treated her in the same positive and supportive ways she was used to and expected, and who whisked her off to live in a big house in Australia. Just as 'B' always expected, and as usual, everything worked out for her. Self-fulfilling prophecies are a thing! Really! As you believe, so it is!

The early learned lessons and messages we receive really do become who we believe ourselves to be, unless we stop and question them along the way. One of my own evidences of this was whilst still at school. Despite continually moving home and school I had managed to become 'top girl' in all subjects at my last junior school. Got a prize to prove it! Then, at senior school I had a very bad-tempered maths teacher who for some unknown reason of his own decided that he didn't like me much, and constantly told me I was rubbish at maths. So, despite my previous excellent and successful record with the subject, I respected the fact that he was my knowledgeable teacher who knew better than I did and bowed to his opinion. I unquestioningly believed what he told me and took his message to heart, thereafter dutifully living down to his low expectations of me. I expected to, and did indeed, encounter difficulties with maths generally thereafter. My belief of my own inability to comprehend, apply and work with anything even vaguely mathematical lasted for many years afterwards! I had gone from believing and effortlessly achieving, to disbelieving and failing. As you believe, so it is. Really!

We are the sum total of our experiences to date, and quite logically speaking we couldn't really be anything else could we? Everything we've ever learned, thought, done or experienced has brought us to who and where we are now. And no matter whether we choose to look back and label our past actions as good or bad, right up until this moment we have handled our life experiences in the only way we were able to with the life skills we had acquired at the time. So, be kind to you and understand that generally and for the most part, your past behaviours were down to your conditioning and learned behaviour. You did what you could at the time.

Now it's time for change. Now it's time to step into your own power. It's time to decide what you want your life to be. It's time to take control.

You can't control the world. You can't control your environment. You can't control anyone else. But you can control you, and then watch the magic happen as the amazing, powerful and beautiful Being that is who you really are begins to emerge! Feel excited? You should!

Every new moment is a new possibility for you!

Chapter 6
As You Believe, so It Is

A True Story Told in Fable Form
GB – Thank you my friend!

Once upon a time, there was a King and his family of loyal soldiers who ruled over the Kingdom of Enough. The people who lived in homes around the Castle itself worked hard to keep the kingdom supplied with essential foods and services and in return, were provided with enough of everything they needed to exist. In contrast, the King and his soldiers lived in grand houses with servants, wore the finest clothing and ate exotic foods that many of the poorer people had never seen before.

Sometimes, tired of working so hard for so little, the people revolted and lobbied the King and his soldiers for more food, better clothing and nicer homes, even threatening to leave the confines of the Castle Kingdom in search of a better life. The King told the people that the meagre provisions handed out to them were all there was to be had and said that they should be grateful. And he warned the people not to be so foolish as to go beyond the Kingdom's walls because everyone knew that there was nothing out there, they would be lost forever, better to stay where they were. Be satisfied. At least, they had enough.

Then one day, a stranger set up camp just outside the Kingdom walls. He bought food, water and supplies from the locals, who were all afraid of him but welcomed his money. They shunned talking with him, all except one young woman, whose curiosity won over her fear. She told the stranger that everyone was afraid because they had all been told there was nothing else except the Castle and its Kingdom. The stranger laughed at that and invited the girl to come and talk with him at his camp when he would be happy to share his knowledge and stories with her.

Later that day, the girl visited with the stranger. She felt irrationally happy and alive sitting talking with him, and when she ventured to tell him so, he told her that it was because she had 'come home'. She had no idea what that meant at the time, but it felt wonderful anyway! They talked for hours about the amazing world outside the Castle Kingdom. Eventually, the girl asked if she could travel with him to see for herself. The stranger happily agreed, and the next morning they set off, across beautiful lands of grass, flowers, trees and mountains until they reached another city, called the Kingdom of Everything. Here, everyone was smiling and obviously happy, and they welcomed the stranger and the girl inside the Kingdom walls, where they were each provided with somewhere clean to sleep and plenty of delicious food and clean clothes to wear.

The girl was amazed and delighted at what she had found. She beamed excitedly at the stranger and said that she needed to return to the Kingdom of Enough to tell everyone. She said, "This is wonderful. Everyone needs to know it exists."

"Yes, they do," the stranger agreed, "You can tell them. But they won't believe you."

Chapter 7
Your Mind Is Not Who You Are

Do you know that your mind is *not* who you are? Do you know that your sub-conscious mind is just about running your entire life for you? Do you know that your sub-conscious mind is basically a computer programme, based upon learned habitual responses, many of which, if not most, are negative beliefs belonging to other people and not you? And do you know where these learned habitual responses emanate from? Logical really. Your past!

Therefore, it's your past that's running your life in the present today, and that is also predicting your future. Are you happy with that? No? Didn't think so.

The thing is, we've become so accustomed to our minds running the show that we don't generally question it. It's what we know. It's what we've always known, and therefore it's comfortable. Weirdly, we find a degree of comfort in the self-image we have created, even when it's presenting negative aspects of 'self,' such as inadequacy, fear and limitations. Which, by the way is far more often than we're even consciously aware of. Let alone those 'down days' when we are only all too aware that we are beating-up on ourselves for not being good enough, but then can't find a way to stop doing so!

We are basically a conditioned bundle of learned, habitual thoughts values, beliefs and emotional responses, that we don't even have to think about to operate in our daily lives. Our conditioned reflexes are constantly being triggered by people and circumstances in the same predictable mode of behaviour again and again and again. This often results in our thinking, behaving and feeling in ways that we know are counter-productive, but even then, we just can't seem to stop, and which in turn, embeds the habitual patterns even deeper ensuring their continuation in the future. Same old, same old. And, even when we decide to evoke change of some sort and make effort to do so, those learned, habitual behaviour patterns stand strong, refusing to budge, and our behaviour comes right back into line with the old governing patterns. So, nothing really changes after all, even in spite of our strong desire for it to do so.

Our minds are computer programmes and having detected early established patterns of thinking and behaviour taught us by our family and peers, they run the show for us with more of the same on continuous replay, automatically by rote, otherwise referred to as 'unconscious, mechanical will'. We humans have gotten lazy and allow these automatic responses to keep being played, even when we feel 'uncomfortable' with whatever is going on. I'm sure you're all well acquainted with the one where your head is saying one thing and your instinctive gut feeling is saying another! Usually your gut instinct and your feelings are proven right aren't they? I bet there are a number of times you can recall having remonstrated with yourself when something you've done hasn't turned out well or as you would have wished, and you can hear yourself saying 'I *knew* I shouldn't have done that. I just knew it!

But, it's a lot of effort to have to think too deeply about things isn't it? It's much easier to simply keep on keeping on in the same old ways. Things are sure to improve one day, and anyway, we can still see Happy hanging out over there on the horizon, we'll get there eventually. So we continue to accept and roll with the rote driven mind programme and end up completely identifying with it, unable to tell where it ends and we begin. We're often aware that 'things just don't feel right,' but we shrug the feelings off and carry-on regardless. Scary!

We live within our given guidelines and our clever minds grab onto our habitual beliefs and save us thinking time and effort in our future, by repeatedly recreating more of the same conditions and experiences. We unquestioningly accept that this is our lot in life, and without even being aware of doing so, we are expecting more of the same and are not disappointed. Self-fulfilling prophecies are a thing! All the while we fail to see that we could step off the hamster wheel at any time. We simply re-act and respond unthinkingly and robotically as we have always done because that's who we are, that's how we think and that's how we behave isn't it? Is it though? Are you comfortable with that? Isn't it time to stop 'wishing' your life was better and 'making' it so? Of course it is. Absolutely!

We are all such excellent students and identify completely with the learned version of ourselves and assigned roles we are allotted early on in life. Then we spend the rest of our days struggling to get free of their invisible but nonetheless real constraints, as we continue on with the impossible task of living happily and contentedly within the imposed boundaries, and failing to understand or recognise why we're unable to do so.

Your mind is not you. It is not who you are. It's a 'layer' of you, often referred to as your 'ego.' It is the created and learned version of you that has evolved to fit-in with your lifestyle and social circle. It's a bundle of outdated habitual beliefs and values that don't even belong to you. That originated from someone, somewhere at sometime, but not you. People somewhat confusedly identify with and believe that their thinking processes are who they are. They are not. They're an outdated old record that you don't enjoy and didn't even buy in the first place, that's being played for you and by you without your conscious consent 24/7!

Your mind is running your life for you without your conscious consent and is using your past experiences to create your present and future ones. It's constantly recreating more of the same again and again. Groundhog day! We wear ourselves out responding, criticising, analysing and evaluating, on and on. No wonder nothing ever really changes for us. Our past life experiences inform our current ones and we continue to react and respond in the same way we have always done, thereby ensuring we stay in the same loop. Going around in crazy circles on repeat. The very definition of madness! Hardly surprising we can't get to Happy is it?

Time to re-evaluate your life. Time to keep that which serves you well and bin what doesn't. Keep that which resonates with you and is fulfilling to you, and let-go or make improvements to everything else. Time for conscious thinking and creating, happy and fulfilled you. Time to start singing from your own song sheet, and playing your own theme tune.

It's what I always refer to as 'unlearning everything you've ever been taught about everything, and doing it your own way!' Which is exactly how it's meant to be! Each of us is different. The world is diverse for a reason. You are unique, and *your* life should be uniquely all about *you*.

There doesn't need to be any guilt attached to selfishly sorting your own life out first either, because, put very simply, you can only share your lovely self with others when and if you have something *to* share. So go ahead and get in-sync with who you really are, and both you and everyone else in your life will benefit enormously.

Our minds are amazing instruments that if used consciously and correctly enhance and improve our lives, but when used unconsciously and incorrectly, can help destroy them. Have you listened to your mind? Try sitting quietly for a few minutes and see for yourself just how crazy your mind chatter is. You'll be surprised and probably somewhat concerned at the constant stream of incoherent nonsense carrying on in your head! A little factoid just to demonstrate said madness: We have between 50,000-70,000 thoughts going on in our sub-conscious minds per day! I know!! That's between 35 and 48 per minute!!! Out of control, complete madness!

Most of us have lain in bed at night, thoroughly tired out but completely unable to sleep because our minds are on a mission to regale us with an endless stream of rubbish. Oftentimes we buy into it too, and spend the whole night awake worrying about something that may never happen anyway. Then, after a short, snatched sleep, we awake again, tired-out and wondering why it all seemed so important the previous night, or, we do the opposite and waste more precious life moments throughout the following day, constantly reviewing and reliving it. I'm worn out just writing about it!

We respond and react by rote to the world around us. Rote simply means mechanical, habitual repetition of something we've learned. Which means that, rather than being consciously aware and present and choosing what we would really like to happen and what we believe to be the best course of action in our responses to the people and situations our daily lives brings us; we react automatically instead, with knee-jerk reactions that are not always appropriate or beneficial to either the situation or any of the people involved, including ourselves!

Did I mention that the sub-conscious mind is subjective, and does not think or reason for itself? No care or consideration for anyone or anything here. Plus, and of possibly even more concern, is that it can hold onto 'wrong' beliefs, even when the evident need for change is obvious and staring it in the face! It's quite scary to realise that the part of our minds controlling most of our daily behaviours is not even necessarily based upon any sort of 'truth' or 'reality' as we know them, and then add in the fact that it maintains a total disregard for our welfare and best interest! Now that is scary! We're each effectively and unwittingly on our own personal path of self-destruction. How crazy is that!

Our sub-conscious mind is a programme, and it's all about past habitual behaviours. Hardly surprising that so many of our relationships get into such difficulties is it, when just about everyone participating in them is coming from a place of un-thinking, un-caring, habitually programmed knee-jerk reactions? Just stop for a minute and imagine how much better and happier all of those same relationships would be if the people involved were coming from a place of care, consideration and respect? No comparison! Good to know isn't it though, that you *can* make the latter happen in your own life. So, what are you waiting for? Better times are coming!

On a daily basis we continue to react in the ways we were originally taught to, mechanically, unthinkingly and un-edited. We are imprisoned by, and identify completely with, the chaotic thought processes of our controlling subconscious minds. We mistakenly and quite scarily believe that this is who we really are. We unwittingly continue to ignore our true essential nature whilst our programmed minds effectively create invisible screens of known, habitual behaviours that stand to block and prevent genuine relationships between ourselves and everything and everyone we know. Our minds prevent us from being who we really are and rob us of our potential. We get 'stuck' because we keep re-creating the same things over and over again. Same old, same old, hamster wheel.

Your mind is running, and potentially ruining your life. Your mind is not who you really are. It is an outdated computer programme that is preventing you from having any real say in how both your present and your future life evolves!

The good thing is, you can learn to override and quieten the chaotic mind programme that's currently in control of your life. You can reconnect with your true, essential nature and find your power, your peace and your happiness, which is right here, right now, just waiting to be revealed by you!

Well-being is your natural state, so remember that when you're not feeling OK it's because of something *you* are doing, no-one else can do it to you, no matter what they say or do. Only you can decide how you want to feel, it's just usually you don't get to make that decision because your habitual old patterns emerge to take over. So when you're angry, irritated, jealous, depressed or any other negative emotion, it's your habitual programmed mind taking control again, until the day you decide enough is enough and take back control of your life. Make this is the day!

Time to re-programme the outdated computer programme mind.
Time to change the outdated record that's been playing 24/7.
Time to get off the hamster wheel.
Time to find you, take control and create the future you want to live.
Time for a new beginning!
Time for you to shine!

Chapter 8
We Are All Unique,
so It's All About You

You have to begin your journey of change by starting with you. There really isn't any other way or person you could start with. Believe me when I tell you that I've tried everything along the way - and it's been a long time! No-one else can do it for you. No-one else can give it to you. No-one else can 'teach' it to you. You can't learn it. You can't 'achieve' it, because you already have it! It's already yours. You've just been ignoring it so far. Not anymore!

In my search for the happiness I sought and believed was possible, I read every spiritual, psychology, science, well-being and personal growth book I could get my hands on. I trained and became a counsellor, a holistic and well-being therapist, a reiki master and meditation teacher. In my desperate attempts to understand myself, my world and improve my lot in life, I now see that I unwittingly became something of a serial student going from teacher to teacher, and course to course. Although, had you said that to me, then I would have vehemently disagreed with you, as I mistakenly believed that my personal happiness lay in sources somewhere external to myself.

I spent money, time and huge amounts of effort in enrolling on a variety of different courses that promised they could deliver what I was seeking, and that theirs was the path to 'enlightenment and true, eternal happiness.' Each time, I diligently committed and applied myself to their individual prescribed methodology, hoping and daring to believe that this would be 'the one' to get me to where I wanted to go. And what I found, after all my years of searching, all my seeking, striving, learning and studying; was that, what I had spent so long looking for, had been with me all the time! Right there, all along! I had spent years searching externally and looking to other people and in other places, when everything I wanted and all my answers had been with me all along. It took me a long time to realise that it had always been all about me. Just as it is all about you.

Don't get me wrong. I know from experience that there is a wealth of stellar information available to us generally, via the internet and social media etc, and I am in no way disparaging the help available to us or the teachers who provide it. There are books, both old and new that hold deep spiritual insights into our existence, and the wisdom of ages between their pages. There are some excellent motivators, teachers and gurus to help guide us through the many and varied stages of our lives. However, whatever their message to us is, it remains only hearsay, unless we practically apply and experience it for ourselves, and even then, our own understanding of the experience must always be a personal one. We are each unique, and therefore, it is uniquely *always* all about you.

Over the years, I left many of the courses I personally undertook feeling downhearted, dispirited and genuinely believing that my failure to find what I was searching for lay not with the course material or teacher, but because I just wasn't good enough, clever enough or spiritual enough. I hoped that, after I'd read my next book or attended the next course I'd have found what I'd been searching for and be perfectly placed to effect the life changes I had desired for so long.

Also, in my naivety, and possibly down to my own generally low self-worth and esteem, I believed that I needed, and it required, someone else's help to reach my goals. I genuinely thought that all course leaders and teachers of my subject of interest must surely have achieved, at least in part, the enlightened state I sought. Therefore, I was inclined to unquestioningly believe just about everything they said as I deferentially bowed to their sometimes mistakenly assumed superior status and knowledge!

Nevertheless, what I learned and now know, is that in this wonderfully diverse world of ours, each of us is entirely unique and will tread our own special path along life's wonderful journey. No-one else knows what's in our head. No-one else knows how we feel. And, even when we try to explain the latter to another, their understanding of what we're sharing with them will always be coloured by themselves and their own experiences. There is no one-size fits all scenario in personal growth and development. We are each unique, and therefore, it is *always* all about *you.*

Everything you need to align with who you really are, make the changes you desire, and find the happiness you seek, is with you right now. Each of us is on our own individual journey and we have widely varying needs and entirely personal interpretations of information. For example, three people watching the same movie will likely all derive something different from it, dependent upon their character, life experiences and current situation.

So, read every book whose title sings to you. Attend classes and courses when they 'light your fire,' and take from each of them *only* that which is relevant to *you,* and happily discard the rest as unnecessary to you at this particular moment in time. You are a vibrational energy being. Get in touch with your feelings and get used to being guided by them. If it feels right, it is, and if it feels wrong, it is, so stop.

Reconnecting with who you really are is a process of growth. It develops and evolves directly in line with the efforts you make. The more focused and determined you are the faster you will progress and the sooner you will see change happen. So, waste no time in finding you. Reconnect and come home to your Happy place and who you really are, and then you will be perfectly placed to move your mountains or make whatever your desired changes are. Find you first, and start from the right place in order to get to where you want to go. It's logical really.

A pilot wanting to fly to Scotland would first have to know where he is starting from and where he is now. Otherwise he would likely fly round and round in circles and never reach his desired destination. He might well stop off along the way to fuel his aircraft and may even have a diverting time in a variety of different places. But, he would be unlikely to reach his original goal. He has to know where he is starting from. He has to start from the right place.

So it is with each of us. In order to get to where we want to go, we have to know where we are now. Whilst we remain identifying with our conditioned minds as to who we are, we are effectively standing in our own way and quite literally blocking any chance of making real and lasting change in our lives, and will probably, sadly, continue on in the same vein as we have previously always done. It makes sense doesn't it, that if you don't know who you really are, how can you know or understand what really makes you happy?

Eventually your recognition of whatever it is in life that's not working for you will bring you to look for who you really are. Because who you really are is where your balance in life is. It's where your happiness lies and it's where your dream life is waiting to become your reality. Why continue to dream about the life you want to live, when you can live the life you dream of? Read on, and make it happen for you! Because your life really is all about you! And, Happy really is hanging out right where you are!

Part 2
Explains How Everything Works

Chapter 9
Our Energy World

I am no scientist, but I realised that if I was going to effect change in my life, I needed to understand at least a little, of how everything works. As I keep saying, you have to know where you are now in order to get to where you want to go. And, also, after having previously spent so much time and effort in my unfulfilled searching, I was pretty well convinced that I must have been missing some important and salient pieces of information somewhere along the way. So, I decided to get better acquainted with the world I was living in and understand how that might affect me on my personal journey. I'm so glad that I did.

Given my layman's status, you may be happy to hear, that I will not be trying to confuse or bore you with complicated mathematical equations and long-winded scientific studies. As if! Instead though, I hope that you find what I am presenting to you here, as infinitely interesting and inspiring as I do! And the reason I get so excited about it all is because I now understand that the energies that keep our world working as it so brilliantly and amazingly does, are the very energies that affect and direct my life, as well as yours and everyone else's. Makes total sense when you think about it doesn't it? If we're working with the natural laws of the universe instead of against them, life must automatically flow with more ease, and if you add into that equation the fact that you can then direct the flow to where you want it to go, you are cooking on gas!!!

In reality, we are each made-up of a bundle of intelligent vibrational energy cells, hanging together in human form which are connected with each other through the components of the universal law of attraction, which is that 'like attracts like.' We connect with the world about us through our thoughts and feelings which generate vibrations, just like tuning in to a radio station.

Our world really is amazing! And so are we! It's just most of us are completely unaware of the true nature of the wonderful world we inhabit or of the fact that the human body is really an amazing machine, with capabilities and potential far beyond what we currently know and/or utilise. Wow!

Early in the 20th century, the general assumption was still that the physical universe was actually 'physical.' In their efforts to prove this as fact, scientists set-out to look for the elementary 'point particle' upon which all life is built, to prove, once and for all, that the physical nature of everything was definitely not an illusion and was indeed, physical. But, as scientists began smashing electrons and other particles in huge accelerators to positively prove their theories, what they very quickly realised instead, was that the foundations of the physical world weren't actually physical after all. Instead, what they proved was that everything is energy!

Science tells us that this whole universe of ours, despite appearing solid, is actually vibrating atoms, mesons, positrons and particles, etc, all vibrating at differing speeds, resulting in finer or denser energy mass and therefore the difference between one object and another is in the rate of its vibration. And the difference between humans and other seemingly solid matter, i.e., mountains, trees etc, is in the information and energy content of their respective localised bodies. Also, we humans have an amazing nervous system that allows us to experience our world subjectively through our thoughts, feeling, emotions, instincts and beliefs etc, and objectively through the physical body. Our energy is such that it can't be seen or touched, but nevertheless, is something 'real' that we sense, feel and react to. For instance, we can often 'feel' that something isn't going well or right for us if it isn't, even when we have no apparent reason to 'think' so. We instinctively feel it. We know it. And at that point we're in touch with who we really are, and being guided by our feelings.

Everything in our universe is constantly vibrating, even objects that appear to us to be stationary are actually vibrating, oscillating and resonating at different frequencies. Each and every intelligent cell helps and assists other cells in their totally organised and amazingly co-ordinated dance, to ensure that our world continues to work at every level. Wow!

Ultimately, all matter is vibrations of various underlying fields, and even when different vibrating things/processes come into proximity, they can sometimes 'sync' together naturally and end up vibrating at the same frequency. Co-operative components all the way!

Amazing to think isn't it, that in this world of ours, nothing is quite the solid matter we believe and perceive it to be, including us! And exciting too, because if that's true, and it is, it means that it really is possible for us to work with and direct our energies to achieve the things we desire! What have we been missing for so long!

We know that we experience our 'physical' world through our senses. People generally believe that we see with and through our eyes. But in reality, our eyes convert light waves into electrical impulses that are then in turn 'interpreted' by our brain into what we 'see'. The same principle applies to all our other senses too, i.e., hearing, taste, smell and touch. They are the brain's interpretation of electrical signals. Basically, we are feeling and interpreting our world. Seeing is believing, except when the mind can be tricked into believing what it sees!

What this means to us as energy beings is that we have untapped energies with almost limitless potential right where we're standing and within our grasp! Hello! What are *you* going to be creating?

There are actually a number of intrinsic and unchanging, accepted natural laws of the universe. Of course, most people know about and are generally aware of the law of gravity. We understand that gravity is what keeps our feet on the floor and prevents us from floating off into space! And, due to the current and huge interest in 'manifestation' many people have become acquainted with the law of attraction too. However, getting familiar with all of the natural laws can help you to completely shift your perspective and change your approach to life.

The Law of Attraction has been well documented, and is currently very popular in today's society. It has a large following of people desperately seeking to create more happiness and abundance in their lives through practical application of behaviour in line with its teachings, based upon the universal law of 'like attracts like.' Which effectively means therefore 'think about and focus on the things you want enough' and they will ultimately manifest. Sadly though, only very few people do succeed in manifesting their desires, and this is because what they are unaware of, is that in order to create and manifest successfully, it is first necessary to be in alignment with the natural laws, their own vibrational frequency and the vibrational frequency of the object of desire.

In this world of ours, a certain energy vibrational quality will attract a similar energy quality. It means that you get what you focus upon, *provided* you learn to adjust your vibrations to the same frequency as the thing you're trying to attract and create. Like attracts like! Logical. And remember, everything including you, *is* vibrational energy, so not such an impossible task as you may initially think!

The well-known Law of Attraction is actually a secondary law to the Law of Vibration. This simple universal principle is the most powerful law in the universe. It is everywhere, always present and active. We know that everything in the universe is in a constant state of movement, which we refer to as it's vibrations and the speed at which it vibrates is referred to as its frequency. The difference between one object and another is in the rate of its vibration. We all have a specific vibrational frequency which we can learn to adjust to help, assist and improve our situation, or to align with the object of our desire, when manifesting.

We attract to ourselves energies that match-up with our own. For instance, if we're feeling miserable and have low energies, we will be attracting to ourselves other low vibrational energies and will keep this momentum going until we put a halt to this particular energy flow in some way, i.e. by sleeping, meditating, or by changing the focus of attention; because, where your attention goes your energy flows.

Sadly, most of us remain unaware of the fact that we are powerful vibrational beings in a vibrational world who create our own life experiences, because we're not given this information. We're taught what our parents, their parents and their parents before them were taught, and they weren't given this information either. So, we struggle on searching for Happy, always not too far away, but just out of reach for today.

Until now!

Chapter 10
Our Thoughts

Our thoughts are real things! They are a quick, light form of energy that is easily changeable and can manifest immediately. They are the messengers we send out consciously or unconsciously to inform and create our material world. Our thoughts are affecting our present and creating our future, and are therefore far more important than most people realise.

Thoughts are responsible for the world around us. Everything we can see around us first started with a thought before manifesting on the physical plane. They are effectively a blueprint for creation. For example, before you can make a cake, you first have to think about making it, then decide to make it (will and intention), before further thinking about what ingredients you need to collect together in order to actually do it (action). Everything around us, whatever it is, buildings, bridges, cars etc, all started out as thoughts in their designer's minds.

When we focus on thoughts, they guide physical energy to flow and, if given enough focus and attention, will manifest on the physical plane. Most of us will recognise the example of thinking about someone, and then they unexpectedly call, or you bump into them in the street, exclaiming 'that's funny, I was just thinking about you, what a coincidence.' No such thing as coincidence in our energy world. You and your friend would have been tuning into each other's energy field at some level, just like tuning a radio. What happens on the inside is reflected on the outside! So you can understand how important it is to your well-being that you keep your thoughts positive!

The same principles apply to thoughts even if we don't take action to manifest our ideas. Holding a thought in your mind is still the same energy that creates on the physical plane. Our thoughts are powerful and attract similar energies to us. If you constantly hold onto a thought about something it gives it the energy that will eventually attract and create it's form in the material world. So, bin the negative thinking and be sure to use your thoughts to create only that which you desire in your life!

There are no random events in this amazing co-ordinated universe of ours, no matter how it may appear to us. We are exactly where we are in life through the thoughts and choices we've made in the past. Although, many of those past choices would have been made unconsciously, through learned habitual behaviour (rote), and may not therefore always have appeared to us as choices. They nevertheless were. We always have a choice.

It can seem hard to say that we 'choose' our thoughts, when many, if not most of them, are purely habitual and down to us being attentive children and learning our lessons well from our parents and peers, doesn't it? Truth is though, we do have a choice. We can choose to 'wake-up' and free ourselves from old thought patterns and re-programme with our own values, desires and goals.

We know that we create our world through the thoughts we think, but we use just a very small percentage of our minds actual capacity to think, because most of our thoughts are just automatic habitual responses. Generally we don't consciously and creatively think at all, we just unthinkingly re-act, and we do this again and again as we have repeatedly done before, because it's the well-worn embedded pattern that's playing out in our subconscious mind. And one which may or may not even be in our own best interest! Help!

For the most part, and unless we make the effort to become present and consciously aware of our thoughts, the way in which we think is purely habitual and based upon outdated beliefs and values that we have gathered along the way earlier on in life. Many of which belonged to other people anyway, and which are now running as automatic responses on replay in our own programmed minds.

We re-act and respond to others with no forethought, care or consideration. We all know that situation where we have re-acted to something said by another in a totally inappropriate manner that we regretted immediately afterwards! Which then left us feeling confused and wondering why we had behaved in quite the way that we did. That's one example of a habitually programmed response, although we continually do so in a much less noticeable manner throughout the day every day. So then, when you re-act negatively, it's usually because you've got something going on in the background that you are possibly, completely consciously unaware of. Therefore, next time you find yourself knee-jerk re-acting in a negative manner to something or someone; take a deep breath and step-back and ask yourself what's really going on. You may be surprised!

If your life is currently not delivering what you would like it to, try looking at your thoughts, beliefs, values and self-image that are playing out in the background of your mind, and ask yourself if they are serving your best interests or whether perhaps they may be preventing you from finding the very happiness you seek.

You can choose to have positive thoughts any time you want and lift your mood. Even if faced with a situation you don't really like, you can choose to look at it differently or find something positive in the situation, or even move your focus of attention to something entirely unrelated that you do like. Your thoughts are creating your future moments! This is how powerful and important your thoughts really are.

Choose your thoughts to create new, positive habits and take control of your life. Anything constantly repeated eventually becomes a habit, so ensure your habitual behaviours are positive ones. There are conflicting views upon exactly how long it takes to create a new neural pathway (habit), some say 21 days and others suggest a few weeks. From experience, I believe that it depends upon the emotional involvement invested in the situation, and therefore also how deeply the previous habitual negative thoughts were embedded. Bottom line here is keep at it!

Worth remembering that the thoughts in your head are yours and yours alone. It's common for us to believe that just because we see something a certain way or feel the way we do, that everyone else sees and feels the same. Whereas the reality is that each and everyone of us sees and experiences things in our own entirely individual way, based upon our character, current situation and life experiences. Your thoughts are all about you, only you, and how you personally see the world.

When we step-away from our chaotic minds we reconnect with ourselves at the deepest, truest level of our being. We reconnect with the intelligent, dynamic and powerful universal energies in the amazing field of infinite possibilities that are our true nature, where our own potential is limitless, and where our balance and happiness in life lies.

Words are the verbal embodiment of your thoughts and your personal power. When you verbalise something you harness it to the natural energy flow of the universe and automatically give it power. Worth remembering that what is said cannot be unsaid, so choose your words wisely.

Change your thoughts, change your life!

Chasing Happy looks at 'how' in the following chapters. Start now!

Chapter 11
Our Feelings and Emotions

Science confirms that we perceive and experience the world we live in through our feelings. Good to know. Except that in our modern day society we're not big into displaying or even acknowledging our feelings are we? In fact, we're often even positively discouraged from showing them, as they can sometimes be considered to be a sign of 'weakness.' Our proclivity towards denial of our feelings, together with our mistaken belief in the fact that we are our programmed minds, is just about responsible for many of us having no clue as to who we really are or what we're all about! It makes sense doesn't it that in a vibrational world that communicates through feelings, a reluctance to recognise or acknowledge them can only mean that we're missing out in every area of our lives! No wonder we can't find Happy!

Many of us are taught never to show our emotions, especially negative ones. We're taught to keep them hidden deeply away, and therefore we become embarrassed at showing them to others or in even acknowledging them to ourselves. We fearfully believe that displaying our emotions not only makes us appear as weak but potentially also shows us as completely 'out of control,' and we can't have that can we? People will think we're crazy! So we become guarded to the point that we deny and ignore just about most of our feelings, and are guided instead by our false and programmed minds. Help! How's that working out?

Even as children we're taught to stifle the sobs and put a 'brave face' on things. How often have you heard a parent tell a crying child 'don't cry. Everything's OK.' When clearly for the person crying or upset, everything is not OK and something requires attention, care and understanding. In these types of situations the parent's reluctance to deal with the emotional turbulence all too often relates to their own inability to cope with the emotions they have all too successfully learned to hide themselves.

Acknowledging and experiencing our feelings is important because feelings let us know that something is going on for us. Negative feelings tell us that something is not working for us and requires our attention, and ignored negative feelings have the potential to cause energy blocks in our bodies that can, in turn, eventually manifest into physical ailments and even disease. Feelings are our personal guidance system that only ever guides us in the right direction and in our own best interest. They are neither good nor bad in themselves, they are simply valuable indicators for us and should always be acknowledged and paid attention to.

Our feelings arise from our actions, choices and intentions, which in turn stem from our thoughts, which in turn, evoke choices, actions and feelings, on and on....We think about doing something first, then make a choice to go ahead and then take action, resulting in a feeling/emotion. And if we do something repeatedly the mind uses it as a pattern and responds automatically and unthinkingly in the same vein to any further similar situations, without our conscious consent and whether appropriately or inappropriately! How often do we dig holes for ourselves!

As a practising Counsellor I saw for myself just how adept we have generally become in disregarding our feelings. In that, I would ask patients how they were feeling about something and more often than not they would respond by telling me what they thought instead. After explaining that I was interested in their feelings and not their thought processes, they would move around visibly discomfited on their chair before trying to access their feelings through thinking about them! Serving to confirm their complete identification with the mind and disconnect from their emotions!

The fundamental difference between feelings and emotions is that feelings are experienced consciously whilst emotions manifest either consciously or sub-consciously. Emotions are a response in the brain and the body to a stimulus or experience, whereas feelings are self-perception, i.e. mental awareness. We are aware of our feelings, whereas it's possible for us to have deeply hidden emotions that even we, ourselves, remain unaware of for most, if not all, of our lives! Our feelings are the conscious experience of emotional reactions. We are consciously aware of feeling happy, unhappy, sad, comfortable, contented, warm, sleepy etc.

It is entirely possible to think one way about something and yet feel the exact opposite about it. Most of us have experienced a situation where our mind has been telling us one thing whilst our gut feeling about the same thing says another. Interesting to note that in just about every instance your feelings would have demonstrated guiding you along the best path of action. And this is because your feelings are part of who you really are, and not the falsely created version of you as your mind.

Currently mindfulness is a very popular practice and system of acknowledging, accepting and dealing with our thoughts, feelings and emotions that is recognised, used and held in high regard by numerous medical practitioners and institutions. We look into meditation and mindfulness practices in the 'making your changes' chapters that follow, and I know from personal experience that they can be invaluably helpful to you.

Our thoughts and emotions directly affect our bodies and well-being. Negative attitudes and feelings of helplessness can actually create chronic stress which upsets the body's hormone balance, depletes the brain chemicals required for experiencing happiness and also damages the immune system. So it's really important to every aspect of our being that we achieve and remain in a state of well-being, and anyway, who wouldn't want that? Happy here we come!

Thinking is who you are not.
Feeling is who you are.
Be guided by your feelings always
—*Brannie Jackson*

Chapter 12
Stress and Anxiety

How familiar are you with feeling stressed? I'm willing to bet you just responded to that question quite rightly, with a sardonic laugh and an emphatic 'totally, who isn't?!' Stress is so prevalent in our chaotic society today that we worryingly almost accept and see it as 'normal.' It's quite common to hear one person telling another who's complaining of feeling unwell, 'don't worry, it's nothing, you're probably just stressed!' Which is actually quite scary because medical research estimates that as much as 90% of today's recognised illness and disease is stress related, which is an inordinately high figure!

The stresses of modern day life today are possibly more prevalent and completely different to those that would have existed many years ago. Early days for mankind would have seen stress related to basic things like finding food to eat, safe shelter from the environment, animals and other hunters, and, basically just managing to stay alive. Whereas the stresses we encounter today have increased and are continuing to do so along with worldly progressions.

Technology has moved forward in clever and amazing ways that have benefitted our society enormously. However, on the back of that and as we progress moving forward, everything continues to be entirely 'new' to us. New technology to get our heads around both at work and personally. New types of companies offering new types of jobs with new skills that you are required to learn and know, whatever your age or abilities. New and fluctuating economies that see companies and individuals soar successfully and then bomb-out. New rules and regulations to live by that directly affect you and your quality of life personally, so that you are constantly having to question where you are at and how to move forward in all areas of life.

Tv and social media bombard us with new things for us to try and buy, and we very often unfavourably compare these items in the advertisements with the things we already have, and then live with the resulting disappointment and newly developed desires. We have so many choices about so many things that we become confused, stressed and even depressed! Even choosing our washing detergent or shampoo and conditioner gets stressful! How do we know that we're buying the right one to do the job? Is the eco-environmentally friendly brand actually any good? We all want to save the environment don't we, but will it do a good job of washing our clothes? Do we really need different detergents for different fabrics? And, is it totally necessary that we should buy two detergents, one for coloured items and one for whites? Or can we save the money by just buying one of them, and using it in both instances, and enjoy spending the money on a bottle of wine instead!

Quite recently I returned home from shopping having unintentionally purchased a different brand of fabric conditioner than the one I prefer and usually use, and, as I unpacked my shopping and realised what I had done, I momentarily felt real annoyance and irritation! Over fabric conditioner! Seriously! And, don't even get me started on which are the right hair products to buy! I have to plan to start my shopping trip early when I'm doing that one!

Stress plays a big part in all our daily lives, whether we're consciously aware of it or not, to the extent that we accept it as a normal part of life today. In reality, unless they are dealt with, the effects of stress can cause serious mental and physical conditions to develop and also often exacerbates an already present health issue. Health issues directly associated with stress are, heart attacks and strokes; high blood pressure; high blood sugar; weight gain, which can lead to increased risk of diabetes; weakened immune system; poor concentration and memory impairment; and a higher likelihood of anxiety and depression. Besides often disrupting personal relationships, along with all the resulting problems that can bring.

Many people today are living with stress and anxiety disorders, such as panic attacks, eating disorders, insomnia etc, and these problems seriously detract from and interfere with their very quality of life. I know about these from personal experience and because of them, my own life became a living hell for some time! And, the difficulties in actually recognising, or of dealing with these problems can often be exacerbated by the embarrassed and ashamed reluctance of the sufferer to admit them in the first place. I put off seeking any kind of help because I was really worried that people would think I was crazy and unstable, and in so doing, my own anxieties continued to worsen and grow out of all proportion, until they one-day eventually forced me to take action.

Most of us today live such busy chaotic lives filled with continuous mind-chatter and external noise, i.e., tv, radio, social media, workplace, family, traffic etc, that we don't seem to even notice or have the time to think about what's going on for us personally on an internal level. Considering we're all we've got, it's surprising that we don't generally think about our own well-being more isn't it? We don't do 'me time.' Quite amusingly, that's something we usually refer to as a special treat! We take it for granted that we'll just keep on, keeping on,.... until the scary day arrives that we don't! We simply ignore feeling stressed and carry on regardless. On a daily basis we continue to exhaust ourselves by constantly and automatically reacting to external stimuli, which in its wake leaves us feeling battered, stressed and worn out, and then we fail to understand why we find it so difficult to let-go, relax, un-wind or even sleep.

We're all different and what is stressful to one person may not be so to another, it's dependent upon our own personal acceptable levels of stimulation. But, generally we experience stress due to either something outside of ourselves that makes us feel uncomfortable, or by what we experience internally when we feel under pressure. Common examples of normal daily stresses that most of us experience at some point, are time pressures and constraints; daily work commute; work pressures; school run; driving; relationships; social gatherings; inner conflicts; IT; social media etc. Life in today's fast paced society is absolutely filled with situations that continually place us under more stress than we are comfortable with or feel we can really handle, and when stress begins to build-up in our system, we can become ill. So, in today's busy and chaotic climate, 'me time' and learning to de-stress and relax properly has really become a necessity rather than a treat!

And, stress isn't always just related to unpleasant situations either. The occasion of a joyous and fun-filled wedding day is recognised as one of our most stressful life events, along with the birth of a new baby, or starting an exciting new job etc, because of the changes to routine and the variety of challenges they each bring.

Having an occasional stressful episode doesn't have to cause us too many problems, but if stress is repeated and experienced often, it can make us ill and so really needs to be addressed. Therefore, being able to recognise when you are stressed is important. Signs to look for are; headaches, tension, inability to concentrate, irritability, anxiety, upset stomach and an increased need for alcohol/smoking/drugs, to name but a few.

As humans we are hard-wired to survive real or imagined threats through our 'fight or flight' stress responses. In response to acute stress, the body's sympathetic nervous system is activated due to the sudden release of stress hormones, such as cortisol and adrenaline. In fact, most of us enjoy some levels of adrenaline swirling around our body, as it can feel exciting and quite pleasurable, like when we're cheering on our favourite football team or watching our children taking part in a school sports day, and there are plenty of people labelled as 'adrenaline junkies,' like sky-divers and racing drivers who enjoy taking it to the extreme. However, we generally find too much adrenaline in the body as really unpleasant, and some of the recognisable symptoms of this to watch out for are, increased heart-rate and blood pressure, rapid breathing, clammy skin, on-edge, tension and trembling etc.

Stress then, is what we experience in dealing with things or situations that we find difficult, challenging or unpleasant in some way. The things or situations are not in themselves necessarily stressful, it's how we personally re-act and respond to them that brings about the stress. It's how we see things, how we feel about them and how we re-act to them. The totally big positive here, is that if it's all about how we respond and re-act, we can take control and do something about it. We can ensure that we reduce and keep our stress levels down. And we don't even have to visit the doctor or get hooked on habit forming drugs or alcohol to do so! Who knew! Happy, healthy, stress-free us!

Better management of life situations that you have identified as stressful makes common sense doesn't it, so try writing a list of the things you have personally identified as stressful, and then look to find ways to either remove them completely or to minimise the effects. For instance, if you rush around like a loon every morning desperately trying not to be late for work, set the alarm and get up earlier in future, so that you don't have to! If you've got a heavy workload, sort it into bitesize chunks, beginning with the most immediately important, and, if down the line you need help, ask for it. And, even when at work or socially if you're forced to deal with that very annoying person who always manages to rub you up the wrong way, try seeing them as the almost insignificantly small influence they are in your life. Limit the time you spend talking to them to the barest essential, and then leave the situation with a friendly smile the very second you are able to! Just taking a little control back, whilst also maintaining the status-quo will help you to feel much better about them and life in general, promise!

Mindfulness meditation is, in my personal opinion, one of the best and most effective tools for dealing with stress, and has deservedly developed a big following and become very popular and quite trendy these days. It's often referred to as being in the 'flow state.' That is, being fully present, accepting and consciously aware, which condition allows you to deal with what daily life brings with more ease, calm and comfort. Doesn't that sound heavenly! It can be yours!

Importantly and interestingly, meditation/mindfulness is found to be at least as effective as anti-depressants in treating stress with none of the down-sides, and has, in fact, been found to be so effective that its now one of the preferred treatments recommended by the UK'S National Institute for Health and Clinical Excellence. Besides also being recommended generally by most medical practitioners these days.

One of the following chapters explores meditation and mindfulness in depth, and as one who uses the practice regularly, teaches it to countless others and has personally benefitted from it enormously, I highly recommend you take the time to familiarise yourself with it too! It will be the best thing you've ever done for yourself! Really! It's popular for good reason – it works!

Chapter 13
Panic Attacks and
the Magic Button

Many years ago, and after a particularly difficult time in my life following a relationship split, I experienced deep sadness, anxiety, lethargy and depression and a general inability to cope with everyday life. It was also the time that I began to experience panic attacks.

For those of you who remain thankfully unacquainted with them, I can personally vouch for them in being destroyers of normal, everyday life as we know it, and the gifters of life as a living hell. They are generally recognised as sudden and extreme episodes of intense fear, causing severe physical reactions, such as distressing palpitations, cold sweats and erratic fast breathing, which occur for no real, obvious or apparent reason. These invisible monsters swoop in on ice cold wings that engulf, constrain and lay-waste the unwilling and terrified sufferers!

Embarrassed and ashamed by the panic attacks, I told no-one, hoping they would go away as quickly as they had arrived, which of course, they didn't. Instead, they grew in both intensity and frequency until they were almost a daily occurrence so that I awoke each morning in dread of what horrors the new day would bring.

Living with dread and terror on a daily basis I attempted to hide my problem from others, thereby causing myself to suffer even more stress and which, in its turn, exacerbated and worsened the panic attacks. They occurred frequently and with no consideration for either my surroundings or the company I was in. I became adept at inventing all sorts of reasons for leaving the room, my office work-desk, transport carriages, etc, and the people close to me who could not fail to notice my strange behaviour, began to ask me about it, and wanted to know what was wrong, as it was evident something was.

Eventually, I plucked-up the courage to speak to my doctor about what was happening, he was a very friendly and understanding young man who I had personally known for a few years. I can recall telling him that I needed help as I thought I was going crazy. He smilingly told me that if I were indeed crazy, I would be more likely to deny than admit it! He suggested prescribing anti-depressants, which I was really reluctant to take, having spent much of my young life watching my own mother battle with dependency upon various prescribed drugs as well as alcohol. However, I agreed to take them for one week in the hope that I would feel better by then. That didn't happen!

The attacks took the form of complete and overwhelming fear. I had no idea of exactly what it was that I was scared of, but the sheer terror I experienced meant that I was almost unable to breathe, and really convinced that I was about to die any second, most likely, I ruminated, at the hands of the invisible monsters I had been told as a small child were waiting to 'get me,' whenever I appeared to have stepped out of line.

During one attack, the constriction of being stuck in traffic on a very busy main road resulted in a swift but nonetheless virulent attack. I felt the panic rising in my chest and finding myself unable to breathe, and believing death was potentially imminent, speedily exited my car with the engine still running! I frantically paced up and down the adjacent pavement, desperately trying to regain my breath and equilibrium, much to the surprise and disdain of the other drivers in the traffic queue, who all understandably, waved and shouted at me to return to my car immediately!

On another occasion, I had been looking forward to a birthday theatre treat with friends, but inevitably, whilst sitting in my allocated seat in the middle of a row, a panic attack descended and held me in its iron grip, forcing me to jump-up from my seat and swiftly exit the row, trampling heavily upon the other spectators feet in the process and completely ignoring their yelps of pain and complaint.

I headed straight for the bar and determined to get very quickly drunk, in order that I would be beyond caring about the attack and might therefore potentially return to my theatre seat and continue enjoying the show I had been so much looking forward to seeing. So, somewhat shamefacedly I stood at the bar necking drinks like they were going out of fashion and hoping that no-one would notice. It really wouldn't have mattered if they had!

Another time, whilst sitting on a train heading for work, I was overcome with a swift and severe attack. I can recall looking around me in embarrassed panic and desperation, wondering if everyone else on the train was aware of what I was experiencing. However, much to my surprise the other travellers appeared to be blissfully unaware of my predicament and paid me no attention. And I can recall thinking somewhat scornfully that they would very soon become aware, as they watched me fall to the floor writhing in the panic death-throes I believed were about to engulf me! I remember fidgeting uncomfortably and sort of hovering over my seat in readiness to jump up and leave it, as I struggled for my breath. And as the panic rose and became stronger, I even contemplated pulling the carriage emergency handle to stop the train and bring it to a complete and grinding halt! Thankfully, I managed enough restraint not to do so, as it would most certainly have resulted in a hefty fine from the railway authorities! Besides who knows what reactions from the other potentially disgruntled passengers whose travel it would have disrupted!

It became completely impossible for me to remain on the train and continue my journey in my heightened and anxious condition. So I got up from my seat and waited nervously by the train doors, breathing in short, erratic gasps and agitatedly hopping from foot to foot. And as the doors opened at the next stop, I sprung through them with a leap that would have done justice to a long jump athlete, as I surprised the poor people that I landed heavily upon, and whose bags I scattered!

I was aware that I would likely be very late for work, but too deeply entrenched in the throes of the panic attack to even care. This particular attack saw me close to fainting and passing-out.

The attacks were adversely affecting every area of my life and I had also now begun to experience difficulty in swallowing food. I was visibly losing weight, which I didn't mind too much, as skinny was in fashion even then, but I was permanently starving which made me even more miserable. In desperation I visited my lovely doctor again, convinced that there was an actual physical problem with my throat, and one which I hoped he would be able to cure. He told me to buy a liquidiser or mash-up my food, and once again offered me anti-depressants. This time, I agreed to take them for a couple of weeks because it was obvious to me by then that I couldn't continue on my downward spiral. This was to be the time that heralded the beginning of the end for me!

The panic attacks were annihilating my personality and my very existence. I had become a rather weirdly behaved, unhappy and strange version of myself that even I no longer recognised. And I knew that if this was how life was to be in the future, I didn't want any part of it. This was close to rock-bottom. And if rock-bottom was worse than what I had already encountered and lived through, I knew I couldn't go there.

I decided that this was where it stopped! Fight or flight? Well I was fighting!

I had no idea of exactly what fighting off the panic attacks might entail or demand of me, but it didn't matter anyway, because I really had nowhere else to go.

Thankfully as 'luck' would have it, the next panic attack occurred whilst I was at home alone. I could sense its imminent arrival, and was even grateful for its well-chosen timing, as this was to be my personal battle and I definitely didn't want observers. The attack followed the usual pattern of starting its invasion quite gently and then very quickly building in its intensity and terror. Sensing its progress, I found myself walking almost mechanically into the lounge and forced myself to sit on the floor. It was a bright and sunny day outside but I felt icy cold as my skin dripped with perspiration and the whole of my body shook and trembled in fear.

To those who have never encountered or personally experienced terrors of this sort, my account here might even possibly read like a work of pure fiction. But, my friends, make no mistake, that for the unfortunate sufferers, the experience is one of pure and total horror and convincingly only too real.

With every muscle in my body tensed, trembling and teeth chattering, I was hovering above, rather than sitting on the floor. And I knew that I was imminently close to jumping up, running out of the building and screaming at the top of my voice for someone to come and help me. I glanced nervously about myself in every direction, terrified to look, but equally scared not to. I was convinced that I kept hearing strange sounds coming from behind me, or saw something moving just out of the corner of my eyes, as I awkwardly and apprehensively jerked and twisted around, experiencing 'real life' moments that matched anything ever created and shown in the worst of worst horror movies.

With a powerful determination and strength of mind that I hadn't previously realised I possessed I forced myself to press my bodyweight further into the floor and remain exactly where I was. I had come this far, and I wasn't backing down now, whatever the cost. I had no idea what that cost would be, but, this would not be my Waterloo.

My breaths came in fast, shallow and erratic gasps as I was held prisoner in an invisible but almost tangible, immobilising, gripping, grey cloud of terror. But I remained sat rigidly erect, as I determinedly waited on high-alert to face my nemesis, and for what was to come.

I had no idea of what to expect, as my mind unkindly provided me with images of every shape, colour and sort of monster it could conceive or construct. But with all the strength I could muster, I steadfastly remained where I was, and forced myself to dive even deeper into the terrifying ordeal. I was in the eye of the storm, and resolutely determined to look this monster right in its face. Despite being possibly the most completely terrified I had been in my entire life so far, I wasn't backing down. I was in this to win, and I was doing this.

As I bathed in total and abject fear, I recall bravely forcing myself to meet my terror filled emotions head-on. I talked myself through the experience, conjuring images and asking myself questions about it, such as how it actually felt to me, where I thought it was, what I thought it was, what colour it was and how I might potentially defeat it. And, as minutes that felt like hours passed by, I waited shaking, teeth chattering and body trembling, in my fear and trepidation for the expected battle to commence. I remained where I was, sitting erectly alert, anxiously waiting, watching and listening, and waiting, watching and listening; jumping at every sound and seeing things move from the corner of my eyes, for what seemed to me like hours. I determinedly waited on, shaking uncontrollably in my abject fear, until – nothing! Nothing at all. Nothing occurred. Nothing happened. Except, that the previously totally consuming and all-encompassing feelings of dread and terror had completely disappeared! They were gone. Evaporated. They had vanished into the thin air from whence they came!!! Everything had returned to normal.

The sun shone brightly through my lounge windows as my body temperature and breathing relaxed and returned to normal. The panic attack had gone. It had dissipated just as though it had never existed. And I knew in that exact moment that the attacks would never, ever, have a hold over me again! I had looked the monster in the eyes and faced my fears, and in doing so I had beaten them completely, and for good!

I had just discovered for myself that the overwhelming and debilitating fear that had relentlessly destroyed the quality of my daily life, and that I had suffered and endured for so long was unreal. It wasn't real! It was a terrible and fearful product of my minds construct that I had completely and totally bought into and believed. Partly, I reasoned afterwards, because the intense and all-consuming emotions attached to it were so powerful that they felt entirely 'real' to me. And also partly because, at that time and try as I might, I couldn't reason or understand how the experience had come about, as no part of it made any sense to me. Which, in hindsight, is now totally understandable, because the whole thing was created by my mind in the first place!

I now know that it is almost impossible to understand, control or effectively solve issues that are created and presented to us by the mind, whilst we remain fully immersed in them. The created mind-made self thrives on power, fear and control and does not relinquish its hold easily, as it works to ensure that it's negative patterns of fear and suffering continue to be repeated again and again in the future.

However, thankfully and even more importantly, I have also learned that it is entirely possible to face, dissolve and conquer the false and fearful mind created self, by being 'present' and aligning with who we really are. By consciously choosing to step into the present moment, wherein lies our own natural and immensely powerful true nature and where ego and fearful created mind cannot exist.

I now understand and know how very powerful and even potentially dangerous our created and programmed minds can be for us, especially whilst we continue to completely identify with them as to who we really are, and as we continue to unquestioningly believe in, accept and try to live by, the created mind's false version of who we are.

Ever since that exceptionally challenging, but completely life changing and affirming day. I have affectionately referred to the moment of dissolving fear, by stepping into the present to claim your own true power, as 'the Invisible Magic Button,' and am happy to tell you that since then I have used it very successfully with patients in many different counselling sessions. And I am even happier to tell you that absolutely each and every one of us has an Invisible Magic Button of our own which is always ready and available at our disposal. It's innately part and parcel of who we all really are, because we truly are all amazing!

There are no superlatives that can adequately describe or convey to you the completely overwhelming and immense relief that washed over me as I delightedly bathed in the ecstatic realisation that I was finally free of the daily terrors and misery that had persistently continued to destroy my very sanity and thereby also, the quality of my life for so long.

The sense of joy and elation I felt in every fibre of my being is simply beyond words. This was to be the birth of an entirely new phase of existence for me. For the first time in a very long time I was looking forward to finding out what exciting experiences each new day would bring. I awoke each morning with a smile on my face, happily secure in the knowledge that I would be able to deal with whatever the day proffered. And, for the first time in my life I felt worthy, powerful and jubilantly fearless!

I excitedly entered into the next chapter of my life, armed with knowledge and understanding of the real power and amazing strength of my own true nature. In my darkest hour I had searched the depths of my being to find and align with who I really was. The real me. The true version of me that lay beyond the created mind, and that arose to valiantly defend me in my hour of need, effectively and efficiently laying waste to everything that threatened to disrupt or cause me harm.

This was also the time that I found an entirely new level of love, admiration and respect for the amazing and resilient being that I was now proud to call 'me.' I had faced my mind created fears and I had won!

The Invisible Magic Button really is part and parcel of who we all really are and is with you now, just as it always has been. It is powerful and beautiful, lying quietly dormant and just waiting to be revealed by you. So do it my friends. Reveal it. Give yourself the best present you'll ever be given. You!

I would like to share with you now, that I left writing this particular chapter of my book until last, because I guessed that I would find reconnecting again with the hefty fears, terrors and anxieties overwhelmingly difficult. I was right. I have shed many tears and needed lots of supportive cuddles, as well as one or two cakes from my exceptional husband during the writing of it. He makes really great cakes!

My tears are not for me now, they are for the un-awakened and long-suffering me that just didn't know then what I know now as truth, and what I am trying so hard to convey to you throughout this book............

Your mind is not who you are. You are so, so much more! Find you, and find your Happy!

In love and light always.

Your friend,

Brannie x

Part 3
How You Make Your Changes

Chapter 14
Making Your Changes

You don't need anyone or anything outside of yourself to make change happen. You don't even have a long list of books to read or things you need to do. You are, and you have, everything you need, right here, right now. You've just never met the real you before. You've been hanging-out with the false and very limiting, mind-created version of you up until now, as has just about everyone else you know, and which is exactly why you're reading this book. You know that it's time for change! Let's help you find out who you really are. That's what the following chapters are all about.

I knew nothing about anything when I began making huge changes in my life. I just knew that I was really dissatisfied with how my life was generally going at the time, and my personal and very strong desire for change was a steely force to be reckoned with. So it is with you. Your desire for change is what will drive you forward, and the results you receive will be directly proportional to the amount of effort you put in. So let's get into gear! The only thing stopping you or holding you back is you. So then, no problem!

There are no such things as mistakes or coincidences. Our vibrational universe's natural state is one of pure orchestrated balance and well-being. Just look around you at the magnificence of our world. Everything works to help, assist and co-operate with everything else. So, when things aren't going your way or you're feeling negative emotions, it's not because anyone or anything is out there to get you, it's because you're not tuned-in to your natural state of well-being and who you really are. It's simple really. Time to tune-in then! Just like tuning into a radio station.

You don't need to give yourself a headache going back in time and trying to remember or recall all the events that ever caused you difficulties so that you can now tie them up in a nice, neat little bundle and clear the decks. You don't need to, and nor would there be any purpose in reliving them. You've already lived through your past, do you really want to dust-it-off and go there again? No, of course not. Been there, done that, bought the t-shirt. Remember, that where your attention goes, your energy flows, and you give life to what you're looking at and focusing on. So, instead of trying to understand why things are not better, just let go and let them be better. And, if that sounds blasé, it really isn't. It's understanding and working with the natural laws to your own benefit. Let's get started making change happen! Read on!

Chapter 15
The Pool Man

A True Story

Many years ago, I was living in a small house on a site with a group of other similar houses clustered around a blue-tiled swimming pool, in Puerto Santa Maria, Cadiz, Spain. It was typically Spanish and very pretty with white-washed buildings, pretty tiled roofs and lots and lots of colourful bougainvillea. The whole area, including buildings, grass and flagstone areas were kept in pristine condition by a smiley Spanish man everybody referred to as 'the pool man' because he could be found cleaning the pool at some point every single day. Armed with his big dredging net, he whistled happily as he fished around in the pool to remove debris and smiled as though he'd just caught a prize fish!

Pool Man lived in a tiny two-roomed residence on-site, so was almost always around, unless he was out shopping with his beat-up, rusty old truck. When not working, he could be seen sitting on a faded plastic chair outside his home, relaxing and smoking strong-smelling cigarettes. He was always smiling, whistling, and willing to offer his assistance whenever it was needed by the residents.

Watching him cleaning the pool one day, I recall my friend saying quite pityingly, "Poor man. This is his life isn't it, bless him." I can remember thinking at the time that he probably smiled and whistled more happily than anyone I had ever known and that her pity was most certainly misplaced and more than just a little derogatory!

Came the day that the owners of the site visited for one of their usual inspections. They were resplendent in smart suits and ties even in the heat of the day, and looked very important wandering around clutching their leather briefcases and note-boards. Pool Man wandered along behind, smiling broadly at anyone that caught his eye.

The site owners were as delighted as always with Pool Man's diligent work ethics and the resulting excellent condition of their houses and land. So much so that they offered Pool Man a new job within their company. He would look after a number of their sites and manage a small team of staff. Besides which, he would now have a beautiful two-bed-roomed house to live in, use of a comfortable new company car, and could at last, get rid of the rusty old truck!

The residents were sad to see him go and hoped that his replacement would continue to deliver the high standards set by Pool Man. People watched expectantly waiting for him to leave and his replacement to appear, whilst Pool Man, oblivious of everyone's interest, continued with his work, smiling and whistling as usual.

A month later, just as the sun was setting, I stopped by Pool Man's little house. He was sitting on the plastic chair, smoking his smelly cigarettes and smiling widely. I said that I hoped he wouldn't mind me asking why he had remained living on the site and hadn't left to take up the new position offered to him after all. He smiled at me, shrugged and said, "I was offered more things, more headaches and more stress. I don't need more things, and I don't want more headaches or stress." And, as I turned to leave, he finished by saying simply, "I have everything I need. I am happy here."

Chapter 16
Meditation, Mindfulness and Being You

Life – it's all about you! The real you, and the expansion and growth of the real you as you go about living your daily life here on our beautiful planet earth. And, this chapter looks at how you go about revealing and reconnecting with who you really are, so that you can live the life you dream of and desire.

This chapter is the doorway to a different life. New possibilities, new situations, new people and new prosperity begin showing up in your life as you align with who you really are and your true vibrational nature, because in doing so, you are working with the natural laws of the universe. And, the natural state of the universe is one of well-being, happiness and unlimited potential. All you have to do is reconnect with you so that the good things can start showing up. Simple!

When you are connected with who you really are instead of the limiting mind-created version of you, life shines on you like the sun! You feel satisfied, eager and in the 'flow' of life, You feel appreciation for everything and everyone and the part they play in your particular world. You have clarity. You feel more sure about things, and feel good about yourself. You trust that things will go well, and they do. And, often, it just feels like your heart is singing! La la la! Who doesn't love a happy song?

This particular chapter of *Chasing Happy* will assist you in clearing your mind blocks so that you can kick them into touch, release them and enter into your natural state of ease and flow, well-being, prosperity and abundance. And you open this door and reconnect with who you really are through meditation.

Meditation and reconnecting with your true nature is absolutely, hands-down, the best thing you will ever do for yourself! It will allow you to give yourself the best present you will *ever* receive, that being, the totally and completely awe-inspiring real *you*!

Nothing even vaguely weird, wacky or 'woo woo' about it! It's not a religious activity, and it is not just sitting down and doing nothing either! Meditation is real 'me time.' It's very simply a profoundly nurturing, comforting and enjoyable method of quieting the relentless and nonsensical mind-chatter of the controlling sub-conscious mind, and finding instead, the relief of the delicious place of ease and well-being that is your innate and beautiful true nature. It allows you to once more reconnect with the deep wellspring of peace and contentment, and your own unlimited potential and happiness, that naturally resides within all of us, and which is our true state of being beyond the mind. It really is your doorway to a new life. The life you dream of having. What is not to like?

It makes perfect sense, doesn't it, that if we ignore a large and essential part of who we really are, it must therefore follow that we only function and achieve, at least half as well as we otherwise might do? So, reconnect with your true nature through meditation and watch the magic begin to happen in your life. Find out for yourself just how completely awesome and powerful you really and truly are, and just how wonderful your life can really be!

Meditation is an easy and simple process, that when practised regularly becomes even easier and even more pleasurable. With regular practice its residual beneficial effects become noticeably deeper and last for longer periods of time, thereby helping to carry you more calmly through your day. It brings a sense of peace, calm and balance into your life that benefits both your emotional well-being and general health. It reduces stress and helps to control anxiety, and has been found to be at least as effective in treating anxiety and depression as anti-depressants but with the bonus of no unwanted side-effects. It produces a physiological state of deep relaxation, coupled with a wakeful and highly alert mental state, increasing mental clarity and focus as it also brings a higher sense of self-awareness. It lowers the metabolic rate and decreases heart and respiratory rates, which effectively therefore slows the body's ageing process! Good to know!

The 'fight or flight' response is something that just about everyone is familiar with. It's an automatic physiological reaction to something that is perceived as stressful or frightening. It's when the emotions take over. The perception of threat activates the sympathetic nervous system and sets off an acute stress response in the body that triggers a cascade of stress hormones producing physiological changes. The heart beats faster, breathing becomes faster and the whole body becomes tense as it prepares for action. However, for people who have been through and known trauma or anxiety, the 'fight or flight' response can become over-active, responding even when there is no real threat present. Stress levels can become disproportionately heightened and maintained, as the poor sufferer unwillingly rides a battering emotional rollercoaster, which can be dangerous to health and well-being in the long-term. Thankfully meditation helps to turn off and manage the unnecessary reactivity and helps to shift our responses into a calmer state.

Meditation and the Brain

There's loads of scientific evidence to support how wonderfully beneficial meditation is for us at every level of our being. Studies show that meditating really does produce measurable changes in the brain and that regular long-term meditators have been shown to have better preserved brains than non-meditators as they age, retaining better mental acumen. Even just a couple of weeks of meditation training has been shown to help people's focus and memory.

Regular meditation has been shown to increase activity in the hippocampus, the area of the brain governing learning and memory, and has also shown a decrease in brain cell volume in the amygdala, the area responsible for fear, anxiety and stress. So meditating not only changes the brain, but it changes our subjective perception and feelings as well.

Meditation slows everything down in a totally beneficial way, and studies have shown that we become far more effective and successful at what we're doing purely by slowing our brainwaves. Logically this makes sense because in slowing down we're likely to be giving something our full and undivided attention and focus, whereas, when we speed-up, our focus of attention becomes split and fragmented. There are 5 widely recognised brain wave patterns and going from fastest to slowest they are, gamma, beta, alpha, theta and delta.

Beta waves are prevalent in our normal waking state and where most people function just about 24/7. These are when we're alert, attentive and engaged in focused mental activity, often with the focus of attention split between several different tasks. Stressful! The heightened beta state of alertness can easily translate into anxiety and restlessness, so it's hardly surprising therefore that stress is such a common health problem in today's society.

Alpha brainwaves are calm resting state brainwaves that are to be found in deep relaxation and light meditation states. They assist memory, learning and concentration and are the optimal state to focus on study, or in making future plans for success. The alpha state is the proven peak state for memory performance, and alpha waves are usually present when we focus on 'the present' as with meditation and mindfulness practice. Extra factoid for you: People functioning in the alpha state regularly are likely to find increased levels of intuitive awareness. I know this for a fact and have found it to be most useful on many occasions!

Theta waves are found during deeper meditation levels, light sleep mode and REM dream state. This is where we withdraw our senses from the external world and concentrate within, whilst we still remain aware of our external surroundings. Theta is the optimal range for mind programming and creativity. This is also where we hold onto all our personal historical 'stuff.'

Doing daily meditation has been found to help you perform better at work too. It increases your focus and attention and improves your ability to multi-task. It clears the mind and helps us to focus on and be fully present in the moment, which in turn boosts our productivity. Company bosses take note!

There is every good reason to start benefitting from meditation now. So, let's look at how to do it.

Simple Breathing to Calm Down and Reduce Stress

First, let's look at breathing as a stress management technique that can be used as often as you feel the need for it. When we're stressed or anxious as we so often are throughout our day, regular breathing patterns get disrupted and our breathing becomes faster, more shallow and erratic, and often we also become a little confused and find our thoughts race off in random directions. Take a moment to just check out and look at how you are breathing now and how your body is feeling, without trying to change or alter anything. Just observe your body and breath.

Next, we're going to do 'box breathing' otherwise known as 'square breathing' to a count of 4, although you can choose to practice to a different count if it's more comfortable for you, i.e., 3/5/6 etc. Just ensure that you keep to the same count throughout. For example:

- Exhaling for a count of 4
- Holding your lungs empty for a count of 4

- Then inhaling for a count of 4
- Holding your lungs full of air for a count of 4
- Then exhaling through the mouth for a count of 4
- Repeat this process, remaining relaxed and taking care not to force anything. Breathe as deeply and slowly as you are able to, feeling the air entering your lungs, and until you feel your body become centered and relaxed.

Slowing your breath breaks the cycle of stress and produces beneficial physiological changes. It helps to slow your brainwaves to the 'alpha state' which is the state related to body and mind relaxation. It allows CO_2 to build up in the blood, the end result of which for you, is a calm and relaxed feeling in the mind and body, and it is also usually just about immediately effective. Also, it can be very easily used and applied throughout your day whenever needed, wherever you are or whatever your situation. Box breathing is an excellent thing to get used to practicing regularly anyway whether you feel you need it or not, in order to help keep you calm, de-stressed and relaxed. It slows everything down and adjusts the pace and rhythm of our otherwise generally fast-paced and chaotic thoughts.

What Meditation Is

Meditation is to 'just be.' It is a state of awareness where you are not 'doing' anything with the mind. Not thinking, concentrating or contemplating but simply relaxing at the very centre of your being, *whilst* also remaining present and aware. It doesn't mean being off in la-la land somewhere, with no connection to your immediate environment. It is letting your awareness rest within yourself whilst remaining aware of the world around you. It is the freedom of living in the here and now, moment by moment, showing up and being fully present in life and being centered, calm and peaceful, which then allows you to make conscious choices, be the best version of yourself, and to get the best out of every situation you're involved in. Hello life!

Our minds are always jumping ahead with dreams of the future, or lagging behind and living in the memory and oppression of the past, but never in the moment, which effectively robs us of the chance of experiencing and enjoying our life as fully as we should. Demonstrate this for yourself by taking some time to listen to your own thoughts for a while. Close your eyes and enjoy just sitting quietly. The chances are it will not be very long, perhaps not even a minute, before chaotic and disconnected thoughts start to race around your mind. You will likely be amazed at the randomness of your thoughts and will notice that they are generally related to either the past or future, and rarely the present. Meditation brings us into the moment that we might benefit from experiencing living life to our fullest capabilities and potential, which far exceeds what we otherwise experience whilst our lives are governed and run by our limited mind. It opens the door to the possibilities of a more successful, healthier and happier life.

Meditation delivers a level of real peace and happiness that successfully tackles and overrides stress and anxiety related problems. It promotes a deep-seated authentic love of life that interfaces with every aspect of your life, building a resilience that assists you in coping well with, and solving problems and the various life issues that beset you. It allows you to look at and observe your life as it really is and to be an involved, conscious 'choicemaker,' thereby knowingly and purposefully creating the life you want to live in the future.

It is a process. It's you developing and growing into your full and natural state of being, and it's the cumulative effects of a regular meditation practice that bring really transformative results. It's like planting seeds in the garden or building up your muscles in the gym, it takes time to establish, develop and grow, so get a regular practice established, and enjoy the benefits!

Once you have become familiar with the relaxed and peaceful state achieved through meditation, you will find that you can eventually retain it throughout your day, whilst continuing to carry out activities in normal daily life. So achieving a meditative state of awareness is not actually against action. It's not trying to escape from life. It teaches you a new, calmer and more peaceful way of life, i.e., you become the centre of the cyclone if you will.

When you think about it, peace of mind is not something that someone else can give you. You can't learn, earn or acquire it, because it's already within you. It's already yours. You just have to learn to reveal it from within by discarding the crazy mind-chattering that is blocking it!

There are a wide variety of different meditation methods on offer these days, so there's bound to be one that fits well with you. Individuals differ widely in the development of their intellectual, emotional and sensory systems, and in the relationships of these systems to each other. So find the one that feels the best fit for you. If it feels good and feels right, it is, and likewise, if it feels wrong, it is, so stop, and find a different path. Be guided by you and how you feel.

I have personally been teaching meditation for just about 40 years, and am still currently doing so, so it's fair to say that I know the subject well! I have found that individuals vary in their likes and dislikes of approaches to meditation, so in classes I use a variety of different techniques and tools to assist students comfortably along the way. What I have learned to know is that there is always a 'way in' for everyone, so when one method doesn't work for one of my students, we move onto another and then another until we find the right one. Check out my website for information on my online classes at branniejackson.com. I look forward to meeting you there!

Mindfulness

Mindfulness is currently 'on-trend' and considered a modern day meditation practice and there are a number of different schools teaching it. I also personally include mindfulness in my own group meditation sessions and have found it to be a very effective and useful tool. It's not actually 'new' though. It's thousands of years old and linked to ancient eastern and Buddhist philosophy as well as even earlier Hindu yogic practices. Despite it's aged-old links, it is not a religious activity. As with all meditation it is a process. It is a developing, evolving growth, through applied practice.

Mindfulness is about being in the moment without labelling, evaluating or judgement. It's observation without criticism. It's about being kind to yourself, and accepting of yourself, where you are and how you are, which does not mean or necessitate accepting what you find un-acceptable. It's about having clarity, and understanding that you do have choices in how you respond to events in your life, so that you can create the future you desire.

Treat your practice of meditation as an adventure, because that's exactly what it is. It's an enjoyable and exciting adventure of discovery that, if you practice regularly, will introduce you to a new life, and one that you will love.

Simple Meditation Practice

- Sitting comfortably, keeping your back as straight as possible. Eyes closed. Feet flat on the floor. Hands in relaxed position on your thighs. Breathing naturally.
- To relax: Tense each body part, then let go and relax. Attention on your feet, tense then let go and relax. Attention on your ankles and calves, tense and relax. Attention on your thighs, hips and pelvic area, tense and relax. Attention on your abdomen and stomach, tense and relax. Attention on your chest, shoulders, arms and fingers, tense and relax. Attention on your neck and throat, tense and relax. Attention on your head, face, scalp, ears, eyelids and jaw, tense and relax.

Then let your awareness scan through your whole body from head to toe, feeling the whole body relaxed.

Finally, tense everything together, then gently release and relax.

- Bring your focus of attention within and become aware of how relaxed your body feels.
- Bring your focus of attention to your breathing and simply observe your body breathing without controlling or altering it in any way.
- Bring your focus of attention to the rise and fall of your chest and your stomach as you breathe. Observe your body breathing. As you watch you will begin to feel much more peaceful. Allow this to happen and enjoy.
- When thoughts occur, allow them to float across your mind as though on a cloud. Let them float in and float out again, without getting hooked into or developing them further. Just observe them and let them pass through, and then return your focus of attention to observing your breathing.
- After time, you will come to realise that you have thoughts, but that you are not your thoughts, which realisation will assist you in understanding that you have the ability to choose to act upon them, or not.
- Remain practising above for up to 15 minutes, then open your eyes and bring your focus of attention back into the room

Ideally, establish a routine of meditating daily for 15 minutes. It can be helpful to choose a regular time and place to meditate, i.e., before breakfast in a chair by the window, but, what is more important is that you get into the habit of meditating as a daily practice, because consistency is what is going to bring results.

Sitting under a pergola in the Portuguese sunshine one day, a close friend of mine told me enthusiastically that she knew how good meditation was. I replied by shaking my head at her in disagreement. Looking baffled, she repeated that she did know how good it was because she had meditated before and knew the value of it, and once more I disagreed. Then the 'penny dropped' and she said, 'if I knew how good it was I would be doing it wouldn't I?' Absolutely, and so would you! These days, the same friend ensures that she meditates every day without fail, because now she really does know how good it is, and what a difference it makes to her life. You will too. Find out for yourself and start today. You can believe me when I say 'the better it gets, the better it gets.'

You already have everything you need to live the life you dream of, and it's sitting right where you are, right now. It has nothing to do with anyone or anything else. It's all about you. Truly beautiful and amazing you. Get ready to be impressed as you become acquainted with who you really are! Meditation is your doorway to a new life. You have to knock on the door in order for it to be opened. So, knock on the door and ring the bell! This is all about you.

Just Being You

How often do you get to 'just be you?' Throughout your days, you're constantly changing and adapting your behaviour to 'fit in' with and meet the expectations of the particular situation you're in, i.e., work, home, friends and socialising, parents, neighbours, family, etc. Do you even know who you really are or what 'just being you' feels like?

We all know that it can get quite tiring and draining being around people all the time, don't we? We have so many relationships that constantly demand and require different handling, and many of which challenge us and drain our energies. Sometimes, it just feels really good to get home, kick your shoes off and close the door on the world outside with a big sigh of relief. Except, and most often, we then have to deal with and meet the expectations of those we live with and who are closest to us, and let's face it, they can be the most demanding of all can't they. Often, it's much easier to go along with their expectations of us, whether we're happy about it or not, just for ease, peace and a quiet life!

Maybe you're expected to cook a meal, do chores, give someone a lift somewhere, help with a project or listen to a troubled friend to offer aid and support, and, even if you're worn out and dog tired yourself and nine times out of ten, you do what you've always done, and behave as you're expected to. Often though and over time, the frustration and resentment you hold onto at other's expectations of you, builds little by little and layer by layer as it remains unaddressed, until eventually there is a personal battle raging within you that forces the flood gates to open, appropriately or even inappropriately, as your unresolved anger and resentment is looking for a home and someone or something to 'blame!'

Allow yourself the chance to bring harmony, peace and balance into your life, so that you can derive pleasure from and enjoy your life more. So that you can enjoy being you! Give yourself the chance to be the best, happiest and most chilled out version of you ever!

Every new moment is a new beginning. You have nothing to lose and everything to gain. So start your meditation practice today.

Chapter 17
The Beneficial Energies
of Gratitude

I keep saying it, but it needs to be said, understood and realised. This is a vibrational world and we are vibrational beings. Therefore, absolutely everything we think, feel, say or do has a vibrational effect. Which is great for all of us, because it means that we really do have far more potential to create and change things in our lives than we previously knew. How cool is that!

Practising gratitude is a positive action that helps us to refocus on what we have instead of what we lack, and which also then, lightens and improves our mood. And, in relation to the universal Law of Attraction which says that 'like attracts like,' the more gratitude you feel and express for what you already have in your life, the more you will have and attract in the future, and the better you will feel, on and on. So start making your lists of what you're grateful for!

Gratitude is a subject that has been studied and written about by numerous people over the ages and has been mentioned in different holy scriptures.

The practice of expressing gratitude as a means to improving quality of life and to attract and manifest desired goals, is currently receiving significant rise in interest and following, thanks to author Rhonda Byrne's excellent books entitled 'The Magic and The Secret,' which latter followed the film of the same name.

I know that I'm really grateful for the many blessings in my life, and I say thank-you for them every day, i.e., my beautiful daughter and husband, my health, my home, my friends, my pets, and of course, my evolving spiritual understanding and work. Each day, I find a new thing or a new way of appreciating something in my life. It just makes me feel really, really good!

As you continue practising gratitude you will be amazed at how differently you will find yourself looking at everyone and everything in your life. You become aware that gratitude itself is a beautiful and appreciative state of 'being' that becomes part and parcel of who you are, rather than just a quick mental thought of 'thanks' that flits briefly in and out of your mind with no attached positive emotions.

As I go through my daily life, I also like to say thank you for the more obscure things, like feeling happy, managing to keep dry when it rained, easy traffic, or a particularly helpful shop assistant. It all adds to the positive energies in my world and makes me feel good, and the better I feel, the better the people around me feel, and then the better the people around them feel. The good vibes just keep on spreading and making even more people happy.

Interestingly, studies have shown that people expressing gratitude regularly are said to experience more happiness, optimism, more positive emotions and general well-being.

They are said to sleep better and even have stronger, healthier immune systems. It just gets better and better!

Doctors studying gratitude found that concentration upon what we're grateful for focuses our attention upon our positive emotions, and we therefore spend less time focused upon negative ones, which is really helpful, as most of us have an almost continuous stream of negative thoughts running constantly through our sub-conscious minds. These studies also showed that simply expressing gratitude may have lasting positive effects upon the brain, although studies upon this particular subject matter continue.

As someone who has regularly practised gratitude, I can recommend that you include it in your daily regimes. By the time you have looked around yourself and said thank you for all your blessings, you can't help but feel wonderful and in a totally positive frame of mind. And, as you consider the many things that you can be grateful for, you will probably realise that there is far more for you to be grateful for than you might previously have thought of, or imagined.

I suggest that you compile a list of all the blessings in your own life that you can then review daily, to remind you of just how much you already have. It can be helpful to attach this practice to your morning or evening meditation, but of course, anytime and as often as you wish is a great way of improving how you feel and becoming happier.

Try starting each day expressing gratitude and saying thank you for being alive, for another day filled with opportunities to create, grow, love and learn. And, also try finishing the day by saying thank you for the best thing that happened to you today. What a lovely way to drift off to sleep!

Chapter 18
The Beneficial Energies of Affirmations

We have an almost continuous inner dialogue going on subconsciously in our minds which is effectively running our lives for us. For the most part we are not consciously aware of the content of this endless commentary about our daily life, our feelings, other people and the world in general. It plays on and on in a continuous stream by rote, i.e., learned patterns of thinking. If you stopped for a moment to listen to your flow of thoughts you would be amazed at how random they are, and also probably not just a little concerned at how negative they are.

Often and unfortunately our inner dialogue relates to old established negative beliefs and concepts that are still influencing our lives today, and where this poses as a problem for us, is in that, this is the basis upon which we form our experience of reality. Our thoughts are constantly affirming our beliefs and attracting more of the same into our lives, thereby ensuring that we continue to experience the same quality of life and type of life experiences as before. Same old, same old.

We use affirmations as a tool to counteract the negative inner dialogue, and to aid and assist us in replacing the outdated old negative beliefs that no longer serve our best interest, and adversely affect our lives. We do this by replacing the old beliefs with positive new statements about ourselves and our abilities, thereby creating new and more positive manifestations in our lives.

Affirmations are a powerful technique that can completely transform our attitudes and expectations about life, even within a relatively short period in time, which in turn helps us to create more positively for our future.

It is generally understood that it takes 21 days to create a new neural pathway or 'habit,' although there are differing opinions on this figure. I have found that the length of time it takes is usually somewhat dependent upon the depth of our emotional attachment. However, the bottom line here is that, if you do something often enough it eventually becomes a habit. Therefore the constant repetition of our new and positive affirmation for at least 21 days, will embed it into the subconscious and it then becomes a new and positive habit and part of our belief system that replaces the old negative one, thereby bringing more positivity into our life. It is generally agreed that the only way to get rid of one habit is to replace it with another one.

Affirmations should always be said in the present tense, and as though you already have or are experiencing the subject of your affirmation. For example, you might say, 'I *now* have an amazing new job,' rather than, 'I *will* have an amazing new job.' Or say, 'I *now* easily release all old negative habits that are no longer serving me,' rather than, 'I *will* easily release all old negative habits that are no longer serving me.'

You can say affirmations silently or out loud, or you can sing or chant them. Writing them down is also very powerful, as is saying them whilst looking into your own eyes in a mirror. They should be used several times a day, every day and said with as much feeling as you can muster! Try, if you can, to create a feeling of belief. Imagine and try to experience the feeling that you would have if your affirmation were already true.

Your affirmations must affirm your positive beliefs about yourself and your life as you want it to be. Remember that you are creating your future.

Keep your affirmations positively phrased. Say what you 'do' want and not what you don't want, i.e., 'I am always on time for work in the mornings,' and not, 'I am no longer late for work in the mornings.'

It's usually best to keep your affirmations short and simple, for ease of repeating, writing and remembering, and rhyming your affirmations can sometimes help you to remember them more easily.

Affirmations should 'feel' right for you personally, so if they don't feel right, change them or find another. It is worth noting that if you are new to using affirmations, you may experience feeling a little awkward at first, but stay with it because it's worth the effort.

You can relate your affirmations to whatever area of your life you are looking to enhance or change, love, work, home, relationships, your abilities or health, etc.

Below are some examples of affirmations, but feel free to make your own that are entirely relevant to you.

- I now love and approve of myself exactly as I am
- I am now blessed to give and receive unconditional love
- All my relationships and harmonious and accepting
- My higher self is guiding me in everything I do
- I am Divinely protected always
- I am now loving my work, which is creative and fulfilling and rewards me well financially
- I am safe. My world is safe. It is safe for me to make changes
- I am now open and receptive to abundance and prosperity and I am successful in everything I do
- The universe supports all my efforts and rewards me accordingly
- I love my body exactly as it is
- I am vibrantly healthy and free

Chapter 19
The Beneficial Energies
of Visualisations

We use visualisations to help create the things we want to bring into our life. In fact, whether you are aware of it or not, you have been using creative visualisation throughout your life through the use of your imagination. Agreed that most often it would have been used unconsciously and without you really being aware of it. But, if you stop and think about it for a moment, you will clearly see that you are constantly creating images in your mind, in response to what others are saying or to whatever you're thinking about.

Our subconscious mind is what is effectively running our lives for us. It's programmed with largely stimulus-responsive behaviours that relate back to the embedded beliefs and values of our early years, and it often and usually overrides what our conscious mind desires. Therefore to attain and manifest our consciously chosen goals we need to access the subconscious mind and re-programme it.

Reprogramming with positive new beliefs eliminates the old negative ones. You can still remember the event and your emotional response, but your 'attachment' to the event is gone. Which then leaves you free to re-programme with your positive new choices.

We all operate from our own unique point of view and perspective, and from where our minds feel comfortable. Through creative visualisation, we can consciously alter our point of view, and therefore change our perception of reality.

Using visualisation, we create a clear image of something that we want to manifest in our lives. So, first, you need to have a clear image of what it is you want to manifest. Choose something that you really believe possible and can imagine having, as well as something that is going to be for your highest good and benefit. You can only use creative visualisation for good and for yourself but not for someone else. However, you can always send someone else love, light and prayers to help them.

- First, slow your breathing and enter a calm meditative state
- Choose and imagine your goal. Be as specific and detailed as possible
- Visualise your goal in the present tense with as much energy as possible and as though you have already achieved it
- Try to feel the way you would feel if you had already achieved your desired goal. Sit with and enjoy the feelings
- You can use affirmations with your creative visualisations and double your efforts
- Repeat this process at least two or three times a day, or more if you wish

Creative visualisations can be used for goals on any level, physical, emotional, mental or spiritual. It works with the principles of the Law of Attraction, i.e., sending out focused positive energies on something, in order to attract and manifest something similar.

Chapter 20
Understanding Where
You Are Now

Often we think we know exactly what we want out of life, and so compiling a list of these things should be easy, right? Not necessarily so!

Knowing exactly what you want and setting your goals can be trickier than you might imagine. We all think we know what we want but when it comes down to specific goal setting, it can be quite challenging. However, the very task of compiling your list can be helpful to you in actually finding and knowing what it is that you really want out of life.

This list is going to help you to decide exactly what it is you want to be, do and have in life. Don't worry if the goals you set now change along the way, that's life, and they are bound to change as you grow and develop. You can simply update your list as you go.

This list should help you to positively channel your natural creativity and focus upon achieving your goals and it should also assist you in finding creative ways of moving towards them. The important thing to remember is that your goals should make you feel great, expanded and happy! This task is fun and should make you feel good!

On a computer, or with paper and pen, make lists under the following headings:

- Personal
- Relationships
- Financial
- Career/Education
- Health and Body
- Home
- Community

Then list your goals and dreams under each heading. You can make your list as short or as long as you wish, though I would recommend that you start with just the really important things and add other less important things that you think of as you go along. However, do whatever feels good for you personally.

For your own sake it's best to keep your goals as simple and uncomplicated as possible. Remember that you can change them at any time.

Be clear, specific and as detailed as possible about each goal, in order to assist you in visualising later on. For example, if you would like a new relationship write something like, 'I want my new cat-loving, 6ft, blue-eyed blonde partner to be a great cook, kind, caring and considerate and easy to talk to,' rather than 'someone nice,' or 'someone nicer than my ex.'

If you would like a new home, describe in detail what your dream home looks like inside and outside. You might describe its location, what the gardens are like, or what make and colour of furniture you would like. Be as specific and detailed as you can, remembering that you can change your goals whenever you wish if you find something that you like better and prefer.

It is also useful and powerful to write your goals in the present tense, i.e., I am now happily living in my beautiful white cottage surrounded by roses and with a picket fence located in the peace and quiet of the Scottish countryside.'

Your list should define and state everything you want to be, do and have. It is sending a clear message to the universe about exactly how you want your life to be, as well as clarifying matters for yourself. The clearer and more specific you are the easier it will be for you to creatively visualise and focus upon your desired outcomes.

Once you have written your lists, I would suggest that you choose just 2/3 things from the list to focus and work on, because if you try to focus upon too many things at once, your efforts will be depleted and thereby also, will the results.

Chapter 21
Resistance

When looking to 'shake thing up' and evoke change, it is quite common for us to feel emotional resistance. The resistance and negative energies are usually from the mind, because quite simply our true and natural state of being always resides in equanimity and is peaceful, content and happy.

Our emotions trigger some of the most profound forms of resistance to change, and our emotional resistance can be deeply entrenched. Usually, it is linked to our past experiences and conditioning. Most of us dislike and are uncomfortable with change because we feel threatened by it, and when that happens, we usually either panic and run-away, as in the 'fight or flight' syndrome, or we stubbornly refuse to deal. The bolder the change, the more negative emotions we may experience. So it may be helpful for you to remember that the resistance you are experiencing is based upon the mind-driven mistaken belief that we can't conquer our fears.

Your resistance can show itself in many and varied ways. You might try and distract yourself by feeling bored and allowing your attention to focus upon something else, or unaccountably feel very sleepy and decide you need a nap instead. You could find yourself suddenly needing a drink or food despite having had both not long ago. Or, you could find yourself feeling depressed and hopeless, and thinking that it's all a waste of time!

The resistance that you experience is actually helpful in that it clearly demonstrates for you what some of your own emotional blocks are, and shows how these have contributed to your avoidance of getting what you want out of life so far.

Allow yourself to experience whatever feelings emerge as you work on your changes. Sit with your negative or uncomfortable feelings, allow them to be, accept and observe them without judgement, and, as you do so, they will fade away, just like magic. Exactly as explained in the earlier chapter entitled 'Panic Attacks and the Magic Button.'

Resistance is fear-based, so sit with the feelings, face your fears and understand that there is always going to be at least some resistance to change, and then allow yourself to proceed and move forward in your chosen direction. Go you!

Chapter 22
Re-cap

What we know, is that we are beautiful vibrational beings in an amazing vibrational world of constant intelligent movement and creation. And, we understand that when we are connected with our true vibrational nature our potential for creating is limited only by our own beliefs. We are all essentially a part of the whole, and therefore whatever each of us does affects not only ourselves, but also everyone and everything else too. We are connected.

Science has proven that our seemingly 'solid' world is vibrational energy and not solid matter after all, and that we experience the world around us through our feelings. So we are guided to pay more attention to, and use of, our own instinctive, intuitive feelings which are in sync with our true nature, and which we may therefore trust to guide us well and in our own best interest, and which we access by meditating to quieten our busy minds and connect with who we really are. Our thoughts, beliefs and feelings are real things that inform and affect our lives and create our futures. So use them wisely to create the future you desire.

We know that our lives are almost completely governed and run by the chaotic sub-conscious mind, which is a 'learned and self-created' version of ourselves and which is based for the most part in past habitual and negative behaviours on repeat. The latter therefore ensuring that our future continues to replicate our past, over and over, despite our own desire and efforts towards change. And, almost all of this transpires without our conscious consent, as we mistakenly continue to identify with our sub-conscious mind, believing that this is who we really are, and as we become more firmly entrenched and trapped in the roles we are playing out. Our means of getting off the hamster-wheel and taking back control of our lives is through meditation.

Research has clearly demonstrated that stress is currently a major factor in up to around 90% of illnesses today, and our fast-paced, chaotic and busy lifestyles serve to confirm that this state of affairs continues to thrive and grow as our stress factors remain unchanged and unaddressed. Meditation is a proven method of dealing efficiently with and negating stressful impact.

Generally and on a daily basis our brains function at the busy beta-wave levels, which is where focus of attention is very often split between a variety and number of tasks, therefore limiting our potential achievements, and which state also easily lends itself to more anxiety and stress. Meditation helps us to have clarity and focus, and to de-stress.

We understand that the more relaxed brain-wave states, such as 'alpha or theta,' are the most effective states in achieving goals, as well as promoting good mental and physical health and well-being. Therefore relaxation and meditation need to be included in our everyday lifestyle as a matter of necessity in this busy, chaotic and crazy world of ours.

Science and the natural based laws, including the Law of Attraction, state that 'like attracts like,' so we need to remain positive and ensure that we only give out what we really want to receive back, and treat others as we would wish to be treated ourselves! We really are all connected, and we connect with our own true nature through meditation.

In order to successfully manifest our goals and desires, we first need to attune to our true vibrational nature as well as the vibrational nature of that which we desire, and then we will be perfectly placed to manifest as we align with the basic universal laws of creation. Meditation is the key to our connection.

Everything we know guides us towards meditation, not just as a spectacularly efficient stress reducer and good-health manager, and thereby, also general quality of life improver, but also to help us to achieve more in life and become more successful by focusing clearly and working from a slower brainwave state. Meditation allows us to access and be in-tune with our feelings and emotions that can otherwise sometimes remain hidden, even from ourselves, thereby freeing us from unresolved angst and it's negative and harmful constraints. And, the calming, beneficial effects of regular meditation grow stronger and last for longer over time, carrying into and effectively transforming your daily life. Are you getting it yet? We all need meditation in our daily lives. There really is no good reason not to meditate!

Why wait to start improving your life? Every new moment is a new opportunity!

Chapter 23
Daily Practice

This is what is going to help you to make your desired changes and move your mountains. It's all about you. The more effort you make and the more determined you are to make change happen, the quicker you will see results.

Below is a helpful reminder of tools you can use. The first two * points should be practised every day for you to achieve and see results.

- *Daily meditation practice for 15 minutes, more if you like to
- *Daily practice of box breathing, when needed or whenever
- Use non-judgement. Give yourself and everyone else a break
- Practice gratitude for all your blessings
- Use positive affirmations to override old negative patterns
- Use creative visualisations
- Review your life goals list often and adjust where necessary

Chapter 24
It's All About Me
So... Who Am I?

As with almost all stories and everything ever written, we'll start at the very beginning, because we know that 'it's a very good place to start…la la la.'

For me, my early years as an unwanted child of a volatile, abusive and troubled single parent diagnosed with some form of 'tantrums,' paved the way for my low confidence and self-esteem and resulted in my feeling generally uncomfortable, undeserving and invisible in the world I inhabited.

Home was wherever mother landed as we constantly moved from place to place. I was an 'add-on', like an annoying piece of extra luggage that is a nuisance but nevertheless can't be left behind and has to be unwillingly dragged around. I learned at an early age to become adept at keeping out of mother and her various 'friends' way. Being invisible had its advantages.

Surprisingly, for one who had frequently moved schools and location, I did very well academically, managing to come top in every subject at the last junior school I attended. I sailed through with ease to be presented with the school's 'top girl' prize, which was a momentous and proud occasion for me as I suddenly, for the first time in my young life, became visible and felt validated. The beautiful book which served as my prize was lovingly and carefully transported home and put in pride of place in my room. I had no one to tell that cared.

In senior school I continued to do well and shone in the subjects that I particularly liked, such as English, art and what was then referred to as 'domestic science'. Guess I was always going to do well at the latter, as I had been cleaning house and even cooking meals from a very young age. My domestic science teacher believed I had potential for great things and asked for a meeting with my mother to discuss a possible scholarship for me to a London school of cooking. I was really keen on the idea as I loved to cook and create, as I still very much enjoy doing today for friends and family. No-one turned-up to the meeting.

Drama was the normal name of the game in our house, like the day I returned home from school to find mother laid out on her bed with a suicide note pinned to her chest. The note lamented her sad, unfortunate life and made sure she mentioned names so that the recipients might feel suitably guilty. My own name was added at the end of the note as an afterthought and said 'can someone please look after Barbara Ann (full name)'. At least I got a mention!

I lived for my books, which became my escape and filled my grey and empty world with colour and warmth. I read voraciously and from a very young age started reading books about human psychology and how we relate to each other and to the world around us.

Quite understandably, for a child who had been denied basic love, warmth and attention I had an unquenchable thirst for knowledge and understanding of human development and interaction, and even as a young child I watched the behaviour of the others that inhabited my particular world with both interest and an objectivity that would only have been possible for someone of my tender years who had known and expected exclusion.

Looking back now to those early years, I can clearly see how and why my life progressed and developed in the exact way that it did. And upon reflection much later on in life, I would recognise that the messages I had received throughout my childhood, both directly and indirectly, and their resulting beliefs and attributing values, were what would colour, inform and shape my future existence, until the fateful day I decided that they really did not serve me well and should no longer do so!

This was when I decided that, in future, I would control what happened in my life. I was taking the reins and starting my search for Happy!

Chapter 25
The Search

As the years passed and I grew into adulthood I set determinedly about the task of finding the happy life of my dreams and the answers to our existence, by reading every book I could get my hands on and enrolling on every self-growth and spiritual course that promised it could deliver the knowledge, happiness and answers I was looking for, and I spent lots of time, hard-earned money and effort in my endeavours doing so.

The early days of my searching in earnest were interesting and confusing in equal measures, as I ventured into territories completely unfamiliar to me. There appeared to be an almost limitless supply of information, books and courses generally available to me, and many of which completely contradicted each other in their teachings. Which one to choose? Which one was right for me? I had no idea. Without the benefit of either personal knowledge or direct experience and understanding, the sheer volume of possible paths open to me quickly became quite overwhelming.

I knew that my 'difficult' early life had left its scars and in an effort to understand myself better and also to make peace with both my past life situations and my life as it was then, I trained to become a Counsellor. I worked locally treating adult and teenage patients both voluntarily and in my own private clinic. Then, later on, still searching for answers as to who I really was and where my happiness lay, I became a Reiki Master, and continued working on my own spiritual development as well as teaching meditation and healing to individuals and groups. After which, and a short time later I also then became a teacher of English as a Foreign Language, teaching in the Middle East for a short period of time and then back home at a college in Hertfordshire in the UK.

Determinedly hanging-on to my beliefs in the very real existence of a completely happy and fulfilling life, I read book after book on psychology, self-help, spirituality and all things esoteric. I researched and followed different spiritual communities and groups. I enrolled on a variety of different courses and diligently and precisely followed their prescriptive methods and directives, no matter what the difficulty or cost to me personally at the time. Each and every time believing that this would be the one that had the answers to my questions, the knowledge I was seeking and the happiness that I was looking for, before I eventually left each of them downhearted and dispirited and believing that the fault in not finding what I so desperately sought obviously lay within me. Perhaps I just wasn't good enough, or clever enough and perhaps the various course materials I had discarded and left behind me in my wake were just simply beyond my capacity for comprehension.

Each foray into a new teaching method or approach saw me achieve a new level of despair and self-doubt, which was exactly the opposite of the very thing I was looking for! Perhaps my nearest and dearest had been right after all when they told me that this really was as good as life gets, and perhaps I should learn to accept it as they and everyone else I knew had. I despaired.

At times, I recall thoroughly enjoying the experience of listening to various superbly confident and inspiring motivational speakers, each one of whom once more lit the fire of my enthusiasm as they convincingly declared that they could give me what I was searching for at last, and that their individual 'methods and techniques' were the only real path to true enlightenment and happiness. But, just as had happened before, my enthusiasm for what they were selling eventually waned, as I lost interest through lack of any apparent progress or perceived results.

I began to question the validity and efficacy of the vast variety of teachings and information available to me. I questioned the validity of the spiritual teachers, gurus and course leaders.

I didn't really know what to think or who to believe. I was confused and not just a little down-hearted to say the least, because I knew that I had previously given everything I had to each and every new undertaking, but nevertheless, here I was, still searching, still questioning and seemingly, none the wiser. Sure, I had gained what I believed to be was some insightful knowledge and a limited understanding about a whole bunch of different esoteric and spiritual teachings but I couldn't honestly say that this knowledge had enhanced my general day-to-day life in any real, impactful way. And it certainly hadn't delivered the full-on happiness I sought. So, not one to give-in or give-up and in true Brannie style, I decided that if what I was looking for did exist and was actually 'out there' somewhere, I was going to find it by doing it my own way!

I now know through experience that for each and every one of us, there is only our own way. There is only our own path. We are each a part of the whole but always remain unique, which means that no-one else sees things or understands them quite the way we individually do. Everything we need for a completely happy and fulfilling life experience already lies within each of us. We can't achieve it, buy it or acquire it. No-one else can give it to us, because we already have it, we just haven't looked in the right place for it. Until now.

Chasing Happy shows you how.

Chapter 26
Andrea's Story

This is the true story of beautiful little angel Andrea, who, after her demise, visited with her desperately grieving family in order to help alleviate their suffering and despair in knowing that she had moved on and was safe and happy.

I feel both blessed and humbled to be allowed to recount and share this very touching and special story with you on their behalf.

Ruth, Manuel, Julia and Lucia's dearest wish is that in sharing their family's story of loss and grief, it may bring some comfort to others who continue to grieve for those they love and who have left this life and material world behind.

The question of what transpires after we leave our body and earthbound existence has abounded since the beginning of time. In this enlightened age, many of us believe that there is more to this world and life than we currently experience or are aware of, and, indeed, that there is another level of consciousness that transcends that which we have become ordinarily accustomed to accessing, and are familiar and comfortable with.

Many of us are searching for more purpose, fulfilment and happiness, and have faith in the fact that they are ultimately achievable. Generally, we are more aware of our connection with the world we inhabit, with others and in our own spiritual evolution. How often do each of us wonder whether there really is more to this life than we know of or have experienced?

The following is Andrea's true story, gifted to us from her loving family.

Ruth and her husband Manuel had 3 beautiful little girls. Their twins, Julia and Andrea were born on June 22nd, 1996 after a very difficult pregnancy for Ruth, and they weighed in at just around 2kg each. Lucia was born one year later on August 2nd, 1997.

The twins were very different characters. Andrea was a cheeky, flirtatious and independent girl, who could wrap the men in her family around her little finger. She was a very pretty child, who was always laughing and mischievously getting up to something with a smile on her face and a twinkle in her eyes. And, usually and more often than not, she was to be found at Julia's side, lovingly protecting and supporting her more placid twin sister.

Julia, in opposition, was a much quieter and a more serious natured girl than her vivacious sister Andrea. Serious Julia had a natural obsession with tidiness, cleanliness and order from the early days of her life, and so much so, that she became upset and cried when the wheels on her toys became dirty. She would often amuse her mother Ruth by tidying up around herself, putting things in neat piles and organising table tops etc, whilst she was chattering happily away.

Ruth recalled one occasion before the twins were even one year old, when she left Julia with Manuel and playing with a box of toy cars in the garden. On her return from her outing Ruth found that all the toy cars had been neatly arranged into groups according to their colour, and she laughed at Manuel for still playing with the toys. He responded by telling Ruth that it had been baby Julia that had organised and tidied them! They were a very normal, happy and loving family.

Then on February 17th 2001 Andrea tragically died in a dreadful accident. Needless to say, the period following this was a dark, traumatic and extremely difficult one for Ruth, Manuel and the girls.

I met Ruth some weeks later, after our mutual dear friend Sharon arranged for us to meet and talk together about Ruth's very recent bereavement. Initially, I marvelled at how outwardly strong Ruth appeared. However, I also understood that she was retaining her distance from the mountain of grief that was threatening to completely overwhelm her, if she allowed herself to face it for even a moment. I recall that the air in the room between us was almost palpably charged with Ruth's deep pain and loss.

We agreed that Ruth would join my meditation group in order to assist her in achieving a safe, peaceful space for her reflections, once she was ready to allow them.

Some weeks later, after one of our meditation group sessions, and as per my usual practice, I asked the group if anyone present wished to share their meditation experiences with the other group members. Ruth, who was crying at the time, said she would like to.

Ruth told the group that during her own meditation she had seen and spoken with her daughter Andrea. She was both laughing and crying at the same time, when she recounted to the group that Andrea had told her mother not to be unhappy, as she herself was happy and well, and being taken care of by family members who had also passed on.

Ruth said that Andrea went on to explain that the beautiful place she was in was not for human beings, otherwise it would get spoiled, and she went on to describe the place where she had met with Andrea. It was on a white, white beach, next to a blue, blue sea, edged in lots of pretty green foliage.

Shortly after her revelation to the group, Ruth returned home and went to look at her sleeping daughter Julia. To Ruth's amazement, Julia was smiling happily in her sleep, and because it was so unusual to see serious natured Julia smiling in this way, Ruth called Manuel to come and see too. Then Julia awoke, still smiling broadly. She beamed at her mother and father and told them that they didn't need to worry about her sister Andrea any longer, because she had just met with her in a very beautiful place, and Andrea had told her that she was well and happy. Julia smilingly described the place they had met and told Ruth and Manuel that it was on a white, white beach, next to a blue, blue sea, edged in lots of pretty green foliage. And Julia excitedly told her parents that the reason the place was so clean and so perfect, was because human beings couldn't go there to make a mess and spoil it!

As Ruth and I discussed the possibility of including Andrea's inspiring story in this book, a butterfly was flying round and around where Ruth sat.

The reason for mentioning this is that butterflies are held to represent souls, change, hope and life!

Below, are some excerpts from Ruth's message to me sent around the time we discussed including Andrea's story in this book.

Ruth's message:

'When Andrea left us I knew that her short life had touched other souls. I had a strong feeling that she was a very special soul sent here to share her light.

Julia asked why her sister Andrea had left us, and I explained that Andrea was born with her as her twin in order to help support her at the beginning of her life, and that later on, as Julia had become more confident and independent, Andrea knew that Julia would be fine and that she could move on.

I believe that I received a very special gift from my daughter Andrea that I will always cherish. She showed me a new life path full of possibilities and potential, that I will do my best to embrace to my fullest capabilities as I do not wish to refuse such a gift.

I felt that Andrea was in touch with God and that through her God was in touch with me and our family, and that Andrea was touching many other souls with her special light.

Thanks to Brannie Jackson, who was also touched by her, Andrea will pass on her bright message, which is as bright as she was, during her short-lived life as our beautiful daughter.

Author's Story

Brannie Jackson currently lives in Portugal with her 2 lovely, elderly rescue cats, Poppy and Smudge, and her even lovelier supportive husband Paul, who bakes exceptional cakes!

She has devoted her entire life to searching for answers that explain our earthbound existence here on planet earth, and in finding the complete happiness and purposeful fulfilment she always believed possible. After much effort and having achieved what she set out to do, it is now her heartfelt desire to help others by sharing her experience and insights with them in order that they might also benefit from these, and use them to create the happy life they each desire and deserve.

She trained and worked in both psychodynamic (Freudian) and Rogerian (Person Centered) Counselling and is a meditation teacher and well-being, personal growth and spiritual development coach. She personally teaches and leads weekly meditation classes, and is also currently involved in developing these online. Information on the latter can be found on Brannie's website at branniejackson.com.

Two further books in the 'Happy' series are currently in progress. Book 2, Catching Happy, which explores the subject covered in book 1 in much more depth and detail, and book 3,

Staying Happy, which does what it says on the tin and explains how to stay in the 'Happy zone' on a daily basis.

Born in London, Brannie has lived and worked in the UK, Spain, Qatar and Portugal, teaching English and leading spiritual workshops and groups.